POCKET
Visual Encyclopedia

Surrealism
Surrealismus
Surréalisme
Surrealisme

SCALA

Contents

Index

Index

Inhoudsopgave

Introduction

Those poets, intellectuals, and European artists, many of them Marxists, who in 1924 were attracted to the magazine "La Révolution Surréaliste" and to André Breton, recognised that the time had come to liberate expressive form, to release the world of the subconscious, of dreams and of 'pure psychic automatism'. They were willing to give shape to their nightmares, paranoia, suppressed eroticism, and to the dark side of the mind. The "surrealism" defined by Breton was "outside all aesthetic or moral preoccupations." Humour, extravagance, cruelty and anguish present in disturbing metamorphoses recur in the poetic outpourings of Éluard and Aragon, in the plays of Artaud, or the ciné poems of Buñuel and Cocteau, as in the art of Max Ernst, René Magritte, Salvador Dalí, Paul Delvaux, Yves Tanguy, Joan Miró, Jean (Hans) Arp, Henry Moore, Man Ray. And while it is easy enough to trace the beginnings of literary surrealism to the death of Dada, it is harder to trace its eclipse: the liberating effects of Surrealism were still enjoyed by the generation of artists following the second world war when action painting and the informal universe offered new horizons to explore. It helped shape the spirit of May 1968, when written large on the walls of Paris and elsewhere was the slogan "All power to the imagination" echoing the speech made by André Breton in autumn 1942 to Yale University: "Surrealism was born to affirm unlimited faith in the genius of youth".

Einleitung

Für jene Dichter, Intellektuellen und europäischen Künstler marxistischer Prägung, die sich 1924 um die Zeitschrift „La Révolution Surréaliste" und den charismatischen André Breton scharen, ist die Zeit gekommen, der Ausdruckskraft freien Lauf zu lassen: sie schweift im Bereich des Unterbewusstseins, des Traums und des psychischen Automatismus herum, um den Alpträumen, der Paranoia, dem unterdrückten Erotismus, den geistigen Assoziationen und den inneren Gespenstern eine Form zu geben. Es entsteht der „Surnaturalismus", wie Breton ihn nennt, „ohne jede ästhetische und moralische Rücksichtnahme". Humor, übertriebene Laune, Grausamkeit und Angst wohnen den bestürzenden Metamorphosen polymorpher Individuen bei. Wir begegnen ihnen immer wieder in der wundervollen Dichtung von Éluard oder Aragon, in den Theatertexten von Artaud, in den Filmepen von Buñuel und Cocteau und in den Werken von Max Ernst, René Magritte, Salvador Dalí, Paul Delvaux, Yves Tanguy, Joan Miró, Jean (Hans) Arp, Henry Moore und Man Ray. Und wenn es leicht ist, in der Auflösung des Dadaismus den Beginn der surrealistischen Poetik zu sehen, ist deren Ende heftig umstritten: die Folgen der surrealistischen Befreiung fallen wie Regen auf die Generationen der zweiten Nachkriegszeit, die in der "Aktionsmalerei" und im informalen Universum neue Horizonte suchen. Man schreibt das Schicksalsjahr 1968, auf den Mauern in Paris und dann überall liest man deutlich den magischen Slogan "Fantasie an die Macht". Dazu kommt einem die einschneidende Vorrede in den Sinn, die 1942 André Breton an der Yale University gehalten hat: "Der Surrealismus ist aus dem tiefen Glauben an das Genie der Jugend geboren".

Introduction

Pour les poètes, les intellectuels et les artistes
européens - presque tous d'obédience marxiste
- qui se regroupent en 1924 autour de la revue
« La Révolution surréaliste » et du charisme
personnel d'André Breton, le temps est venu
de libérer l'expression en la laissant vagabonder
dans les territoires de l'inconscient, du rêve et
des automatismes psychiques, afin de donner
forme aux cauchemars, aux paranoïas, à
l'érotisme refoulé, aux associations d'idées et
aux fantasmes de l'esprit - à tous « ces faits dont
je n'arrive à être pour moi-même que le témoin
hagard » (Nadja). Naît ainsi le «surnaturalisme »
tel que le définit Breton, « au-delà de toute
préoccupation esthétique et morale ». Humour,
inventivité débridée, angoisse et cruauté se
mêlent aux métamorphoses déconcertantes
d'entités protéiformes, récurrentes dans les
fulgurances poétiques d'Éluard ou d'Aragon, dans
les pièces théâtrales d'Artaud, dans les poèmes
cinématographiques de Buñuel et de Cocteau,
et dans les œuvres plastiques de Max Ernst, René
Magritte, Salvador Dalí, Paul Delvaux, Yves Tanguy,
Joan Miró, Jean (Hans) Arp, Henry Moore et Man
Ray - pour ne citer que les plus célèbres. Il est assez
facile de s'entendre sur une date de départ pour
la poétique surréaliste, avec les funérailles de Dada
(1923), mais cet accord devient beaucoup plus
délicat quand il s'agit de déterminer le moment de
l'épilogue : les effets de la « libération surréaliste »
se feront longtemps sentir sur les générations de
la deuxième après-guerre, qui trouveront dans la
« peinture d'action » et dans l'univers informel
les nouveaux horizons de leurs recherches. On
arrive ainsi jusqu'au fatidique « mai 68 » où l'on
voit fleurir sur les murs de Paris (puis d'ailleurs)
un slogan magique… et surréaliste dans toutes
les acceptions du terme : « L'imagination au
pouvoir ! ». On se rappelle alors les formules
incisives du discours ravageur prononcé par Breton
à l'université de Yale en 1942 : « Le surréalisme
est né de l'affirmation d'une foi sans limite dans le
génie de la jeunesse ».

Introductie

Voor de dichters, intellectuelen en Europese
kunstenaars, meestal met een marxistische
overtuiging, die zich in 1924 rondom het tijdschrift
"La Révolution Surrévolution Surréalista" en
het charisma van André Breton opstellen, is de
tijd gekomen om zich ongeremd te uiten, door
onvoorwaardelijk te dwalen in de gebieden
van het onderbewustzijn, de droom en het
psychisch automatisme, om vorm te geven aan de
nachtmerries, de paranoia, de onderdrukte erotiek,
de mentale associaties en de fantasiebeelden van
de geest. Het "surnaturalisme", zoals het genoemd
wordt door Breton, is geboren "zonder enkele
esthetische en morele zorg". Humor, onmetelijke
inspiratie, wreedheid en angst doen zich voor bij
de verwarrende metamorfoses van veelvormige
individuen, die we terug vinden in de schitterende
poëtische teksten van Éluard of Aragon, in de
theatrale pièces van Artaud, in de beeldende
poëzie van Buñuel en Cocteau en in de werken
van Max Ernst, René Magritte, Salvador Dalí, Paul
Delvaux, Yves Tanguy, Joan Miró, Jean (Hans) Arp,
Henry Moore en Man Ray. En zoals het begin
van de surrealistische poëtica gemakkelijk is te
herleiden tot na de doodverklaring van Dada, zo is
het bepalen van het einde omstreden: de effecten
van de surrealistische bevrijding vielen over de
generaties van na de Tweede Wereldoorlog, die
in "Action Painting" en in de informele wereld
nieuwe horizonnen vonden. De doorslag wordt
gegeven in mei 1968, wanneer op de muren van
Parijs en daarna overal de magische slogan "De
verbeelding aan de macht" prijkt. Met dit doel
komt de doeltreffende openingsrede in gedachte,
die door André Breton in de herfst van 1942 wordt
gehouden aan de Yale University: "Het surrealisme
is ontstaan vanuit een bevestiging van grenzeloos
geloof in de genie van de jeugd".

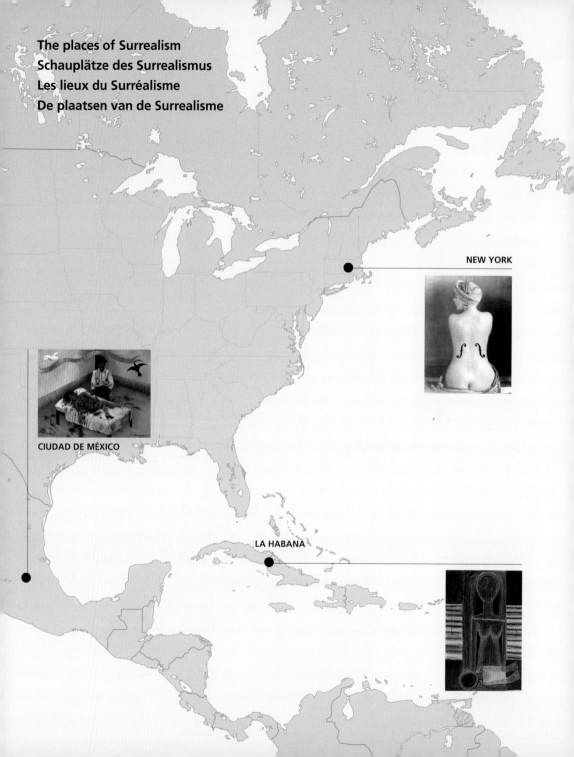

The places of Surrealism
Schauplätze des Surrealismus
Les lieux du Surréalisme
De plaatsen van de Surrealisme

NEW YORK

CIUDAD DE MÉXICO

LA HABANA

LONDON

BERLIN

BRUSSEL

PARIS

ZURICH

BARCELONA

The great masters of Surrealism
Vertreter des Surrealismus
Les protagonistes de Surréalisme
De protagonisten van de Surrealisme

| 1880 | 1890 | 1900 | 1910 | 1920 | 1930 |

Francis Picabia
1879

*Idylle : La ville et mer amoureux / Idyll: Stadt- und Meer verliebt /
Idylle / Idylle de stad en de zee verliefd*
1927
Musée des Beaux Arts, Grenoble

Man Ray
1890

*Present / Geschenk /
Cadeau / Het geschenk*
1921
Museum of Modern Art , New York

1891

Joan Miró
1893

*Animated landscape / Belebte Landschaft /
Paysage animé / Bezield landschap (Animated landscape)*
1927
Metropolitan Museum of Art, New York

1897

René Magritte
1898

Yves Tanguy
1900

Salvador Dalí
1904

1940   **1950**   **1960**   **1970**   **1980**   **1990**

1953

1976

Max Ernst 1976

Napoleon in the desert / Napoleon in der Wildnis /
Napoléon dans le désert / Napoleon in de wildernis
1941
Museum of Modern Art, New York

1983

The stairway / Die Treppe /
L'Escalier / De trap
1946
Museum voor Schone Kunsten, Gand

Paul Delvaux 1994

Le retour / Der Rückweg /
De terugkeer (Le retour)
1940
Musées Royaux des Beaux-Arts, Brussel

1967

1955

Imaginary number / Imaginäre Zahlen /
Nombres imaginaires / Imaginair nummer
1954
Museo Thyssen-Bornemisza, Madrid

1989

Soft construction with boiled beans (Premonition of the Civil War) / Weiche Konstruktion
mit gekochten Bohnen / Construction molle avec haricots bouillis (Prémonition de la guerre
civile) / Weke constructie met gekookte bonen (Voorgevoel van de Burgeroorlog)
1936
Philadelphia Museum of Art, Philadelphia

The laws of chance

It was the French writer and poet André Breton, a great admirer of the psychoanalytical theories of Sigmund Freud, who drew up the first Surrealist Manifesto in 1924. Art took on the role of expressing what lay hidden in the unconscious, through "pure psychic automatism". The artist must leave his thoughts to wander, be rid of inhibitions, and combine ideas, words and images in free and casual association.

Die Gestze des Zufalls

Der französische Literat André Breton schätzt die psychoanalytischen Theorien Sigmund Freuds und verfasst 1924 das Erste Manifest des Surrealismus. Demnach besteht die Rolle der Kunst darin, durch Prozesse eines "reinen psychischen Automatismus" das auszudrücken, was sich im Unterbewusstsein verbirgt. Der Künstler lässt den Gedanken schweifen, hebt die hemmenden Hindernisse auf, sammelt Ideen, Worte, Bilder und stellt sie in freien, zufälligen Assoziationen zusammen.

Les lois du hasard

C'est l'écrivain français André Breton - lecteur enthousiaste des théories psychanalytiques de Sigmund Freud - qui signe en 1924 le premier Manifeste du Surréalisme. Le rôle de l'art est donc d'exprimer ce qui se cache dans l'inconscient, à travers les procédés de « l'automatisme psychique pur ». L'artiste doit laisser vagabonder sa pensée, supprimer les entraves de toute inhibition et recueillir les idées, les images et les paroles désormais assemblées dans la contingence d'associations libres.

De wetten van het toeval

De Franse letterkundige André Breton, bewonderaar van de psychoanalytische theorie van Sigmund Freud, publiceerde in 1924 het eerste Manifest van het Surrealisme. De rol van kunst is het uitdrukken van datgene wat onstaat in het onderbewustzijn, door middel van processen van "puur psychisch automatisme". De kunstenaar laat zijn gedachten de vrije loop, gooit alle remmen los en brengt ideeën, woorden en beelden, samengesteld uit vrije en toevallige associaties, bijeen.

1

Masterpieces of Surrealism
Sehenswerte der Surrealismus
Chefs-d'œuvre du Surréalisme
Meesterwerken van de Surrealisme

Max Ernst
Ubu imperator
1923
Centre Georges Pompidou, Musée
National d'art Moderne, Paris

René Magritte
The betrayal of images
Der Verrat der Bilder
La Trahison des images
Het verraad van de beelden
1929
County Museum of Art, Los Angeles

1920   **1925**   **1930**   **1935**

Francis Picabia
Les seins
Die Brüste
De boezem
1924
Private Collection / Privatsammlung /
Collection privée / Privécollectie

Salvador Dalí
Partial hallucination: six apparitions of Lenin on a Grand Piano
Partielle Sinnestäuschung: Sechs Erscheinungen Lenins auf dem Flügel
Hallucination partielle : six images de Lénine sur un piano
Gedeeltelijke hallucinatie: zes verschijningen van Lenin op een vleugelpiano
1931
Centre Georges Pompidou, Musée National d'Art Moderne, Paris

André Masson
Labyrinth
Das Labyrinth
Le Labyrinthe
Het labyrint
1938
Centre Georges Pompidou, Musée
National d'Art Moderne, Paris

Alberto Giacometti
Cart
Der Wagen
Char
Wagen
1950
Museum of Modern Art, New York

1940　　　**1945**　　　**1950**　　　**1955**　　　**1960**

Joan Miró
Constellation: before the rainbow
Konstellation: Gegenüber dem Regenbogen
Constellation : face à l'arc-en-ciel
Constellatie: naar de regenboog
1941
Metropolitan Museum of Art, New York

Yves Tanguy
From green to white
Von Grün zu Weiss
Du vert au blanc
Van groen naar wit
1954
Metropolitan Museum of Art, New York

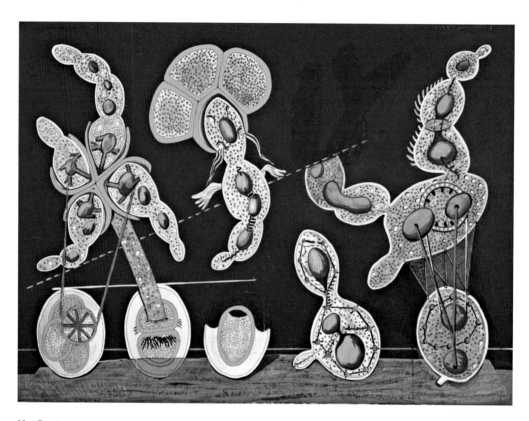

Max Ernst
(Brühl 1891 - Paris 1976)
The Gramineous Bicycle Garnished with Bells the Dappled Fire Damps and the Echinoderms Bending the Spine to Look for Caresses,
gouache, ink, and pencil on printed paper on paperboard
Das Gramineafahrrad verziert mit Glocken, Feuerflecken und Stachelhäuter die sich für Zärtlichkeiten beugen,
botanische Tafel mit Gouache verändert
La Bicyclette graminée garnie de grelots, les grisons grivelés et les échinodermes courbant l'échine pour quêter des caresses,
planches botaniques modifiées à la gouache
De kruidachtige fiets versierd met bellen dooft het opgerakelde vuur en de stekelhuidigen buigen hun stekels om gestreeld te worden,
botanische panelen gewijzigd met gouache
1920-1921
74,3 x 99,7 cm / 29.2 x 39.2 in.
Museum of Modern Art, New York

▶ **Max Ernst**
(Brühl 1891 - Paris 1976)
Ubu imperator
Oil on canvas
Öl auf Leinwand
Huile sur toile
Olieverf op doek
1923
81 x 65 cm / 31.8 x 25.5 in.
Centre Georges Pompidou, Musée National d'Art Moderne, Paris

Joan Miró
(Barcelona 1893 - Palma de Mallorca 1983)
Horse, pipe and red flower, oil on canvas
Pferd, Pfeife und eine rote Blume, Öl auf Leinwand
Cheval, pipe et fleur rouge, huile sur toile
Paard, pijp en rode bloem, olieverf op doek
1920
82,6 x 74,9 cm / 32.5 x 29.4 in.
Philadelphia Museum of Art, Philadelphia

▶ **Max Ernst**
(Brühl 1891 - Paris 1976)
Ambiguous Figures, pencil, pen and ink, wash, gouache, collage
Zweideutige Figur, Bleistift, Tusche, Aquarell, Gouache, Collage
Figures ambiguës, mine de plomb, plume et encre de chine, aquarelle,
gouache, collage
Ambigue Figuren, potlood, pen en chinese inkt, aquarel, gouache, collage
1919-1920
40 x 33 cm / 15.7 x 12.9 in.
Kupferstichkabinett, Staatliche Museen zu Berlin, Berlin

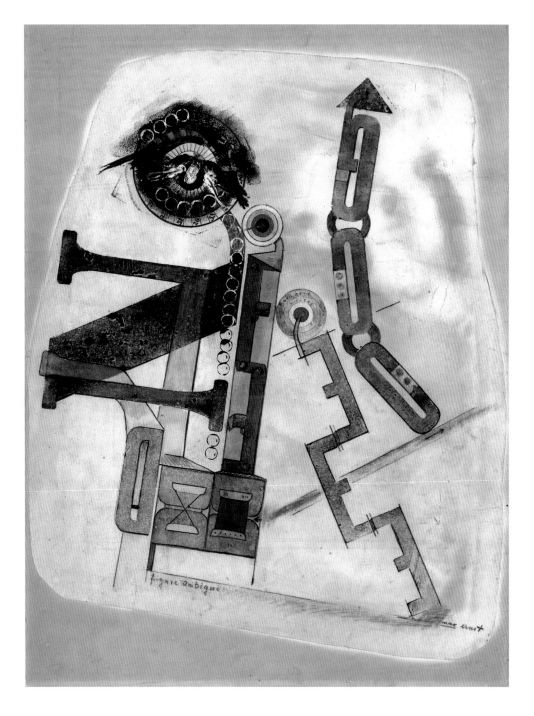

figure ambiguë

max ernst

Joan Miró
(Barcelona 1893 - Palma de Mallorca 1983)
The Kerosene lamp, oil on canvas
Öllampe, Öl auf Leinwand
Lampe à carbure, huile sur toile
De carbietlamp, olieverf op doek
1922-1923
38,1 x 45,7 cm / 14.9 x 17.9 in.
Museum of Modern Art, New York

▶ **Man Ray**
(Philadelphia 1890 - Paris 1976)
Compass, gelatin silver print
Kompass, Gelatine Silbersalz-Druck
Compass, épreuve gélatino-argentique
Kompas, gelatinezilverafdruk
1920
11,7 x 8,6 cm / 4.6 x 3.3 in.
Museum of Modern Art, New York

Man Ray
(Philadelphia 1890 - Paris 1976)
Chess pieces, silver-plated and oxidized
Schachfiguren, versilbertes Messing
Jeu d'échecs, silver plated brass
Schaakstukken, verzilverd en geoxideerd
1920-1925
h. 7 cm / 2.7 in.
Museum of Modern Art, New York

◀ **Man Ray**
(Philadelphia 1890 - Paris 1976)
Lampshade, painted metal on a wood base
Lampenschirm, bemaltes Metal auf Holzuntergrund
Lampshade, métal peint sur un support de bois
Lampenkap, beschilderd metaal op houten voetstuk
1921
115,3 x 7,7 cm / 45.3 x 3 in.
Yale University Art Gallery, New Haven

Francis Picabia
(Paris 1879 - 1953)
Udnie (ou la danse), oil on canvas
Udnie (oder der Tanz), Öl auf Leinwand
Udnie. Jeune fille américaine ; Danse, huile sur toile
Udnie (of de dans), olieverf op doek
1913
300 x 300 cm / 118.1 x 118.1 in.
Centre Georges Pompidou, Musée National d'Art Moderne, Paris

Francis Picabia
(Paris 1879 - 1953)
Comic Wedlock, oil on canvas
Komische Hochzeit, Öl auf Leinwand
Mariage comique, huile sur toile
Komisch huwelijk, olieverf op doek
1914
196,5 x 200 cm / 77.3 x 118 in.
Museum of Modern Art, New York

Yves Tanguy
(Paris 1900 - Woodbury, CT. 1955)
Joan Miró
(Barcelona 1893 - Palma de Mallorca 1983)
Max Morise
(Paris 1900 - 1973)
Man Ray
(Philadelphia 1890 - Paris 1976)
'Exquisite Corpse': Nude, Composite drawing: pen and ink, pencil, and colored crayon on paper
'Cadavre exquis': Akt, Zusammengesetzte Zeichnung: Feder und Tinte, Blei- und Farbstift auf Papier
'Cadavre exquis': nu. Dessin composite : plume et encre, crayon et crayons de couleur sur papier
'Cadavre exquis': Naakt, samengestelde tekening: pen en inkt, potlood en kleurpotlood op papier
1926 -1927
36,2 x 22 cm / 14.2 x 8.6 in.
Museum of Modern Art, New York

◀ **Paul Éluard**
(Saint-Denis 1895 - Charenton-le-Pont 1952)
Nush Éluard
(Mulhouse 1906 - Paris 1946)
Valentine Hugo
(Boulogne-sur-Mer 1887 - Paris 1968)
André Breton
(Tinchebray 1896 - Paris 1966)
Exquisite Corpse
Cadavre exquis
Ausgezeichneter Kadaver
Cadavre exquis (voorbeeldig lijk)
c.1934
Musée d'Art et d'Histoire, Saint Denis

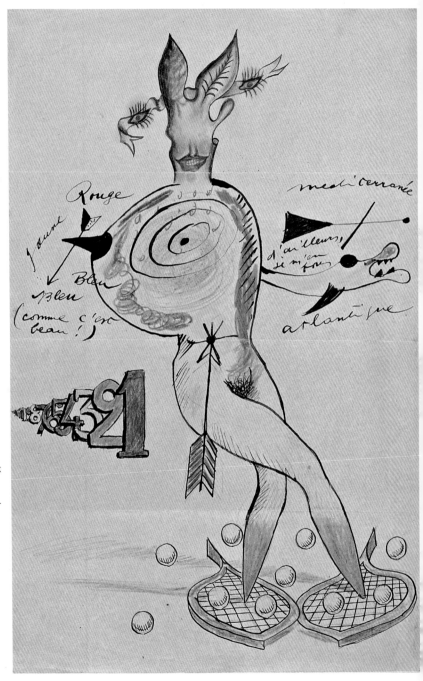

Jean (Hans) Arp
(Strasbourg 1887 - Basel 1966)
Mountain, Navel, Anchors, Table, gouache on board
with cut-outs
Berg, Tisch, Anker und Nabel, Gouache auf Pappe
mit ausgeschnittenen Teilen
Nature morte : Montagne, Table, Ancre et Nombril,
gouache sur carton avec éléments retaillés
Berg, tafel, ankers en navel, gouache op karton met
uitgesneden elementen
1925
75,2 x 59,7 cm / 29.6 x 23.5 in.
Museum of Modern Art, New York

▶ **Jean (Hans) Arp**
(Strasbourg 1887 - Basel 1966)
Eyes, nose, moustache, irregular shapes painted on
board, glass panels and a silver frame
Augen, Nase, Schnurrbart, Karton unregelmäßig
bemalt, mit Glasschichten und grauem Rahmen
Yeux, nez, moustaches, carton peint, de forme
irrégulière, avec plaques de verre et cadre gris
Ogen, neus, snor, beschilderd karton in
onregelmatige vorm, glasplaten en grijze lijst
1928
51 x 38,7 cm / 20 x 15.2 in.
Hamburger Kunsthalle, Hamburg

Jean (Hans) Arp
(Strasbourg 1887 - Basel 1966)
Objects arranged according to the laws of chance, relief in wood
Gegenstände aufgestellt nach den Gesetzen des Zufalls, Holzrelief
Objets disposés selon la loi du hasard, relief en bois
Objecten gearrangeerd volgens de wetten van het toeval, houten reliëf
1930
26,3 x 28,3 x 5,4 cm / 10.3 x 11.1 x 2.1 in.
Museum of Modern Art, New York

▶ **Jean (Hans) Arp**
(Strasbourg 1887 - Basel 1966)
Constellation, painted wood
Konstellation, bemaltes Holz
Constellation, bois peint
Constellatie, beschilderd hout
1932
29,6 x 33,1 x 6 cm / 11.6 x 13 x 2.3 in.
Museum of Modern Art, New York

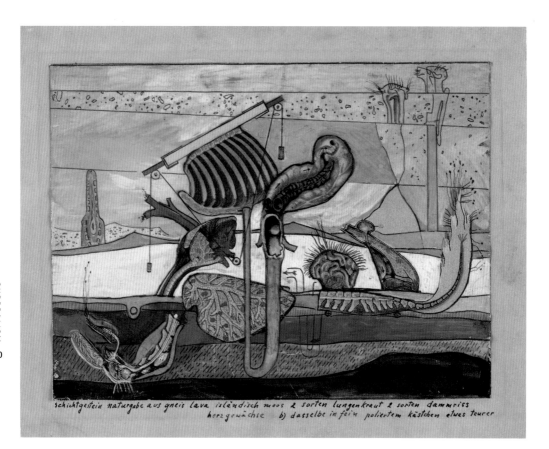

Max Ernst
(Brühl 1891 - Paris 1976)
Stratified Rocks, Nature's Gift of Gneiss Lava Iceland Moss, gouache and pencil on printed paper on cardstock
Schichtgestein, Naturgabe aus Gneis, Lava, isländisches Moos, 2 Sorten Lungenkraut, 2 Sorten Dammriss, Herzgewächse, b) dasselbe in fein poliertem Kästchen etwas teurer, Gouache und Bleistift auf Pappe mit Federinschriften
Roches stratifiées, cadeau naturel de la lave gneiss, mousse islandaise, deux types de poumons, deux types de hernies périnéales, excroissances du cœur la même chose dans une petite boîte bien polie, un peu plus cher, gouache et mine de plomb sur chromolithographie montée sur carton, avec des inscriptions à la plume (en allemand)
Gelaagd gesteente, een geschenk van de natuur van gneiss, lava, IJslands mos, twee soorten scheuringen van het perinaeum een vergroot hart hetzelfde in een iets duurdere mooi glimmende doos, kleurenlitho met gouache en potlood op bordkarton met inscripties met pen
1920
15,2 x 20,6 cm / 5.9 x 8.1 in.
Museum of Modern Art, New York

Max Ernst
(Brühl 1891 - Paris 1976)
The small tear duct that says tic tac (La petite fistule lacrymale qui dit tic tac), pencil and ink on wallpaper mounted on panel
Die kleine Tränenfistel sagt tic tac (mit Inschrift: La petite fistule lacymale qui dit tic tac), Bleistift und Tinte auf Tapete aufgetragen auf Holz
La Petite Fistule lacrymale qui dit tic tac, mine de plomb et encre sur papier peint marouflé sur bois
De kleine traanklier die tik-tak zegt (met inscriptie: La petite fistule lacrymale qui dit tic tac), gesjabloneerd behang met potlood en inkt op paneel
1920
37,9 x 25 cm / 14.9 x 9.8 in.
Museum of Modern Art, New York

Man Ray
(Philadelphia 1890 - Paris 1976)
Rayograph (film coils), gelatin silver print
Fotogramm (Foliespiralen), Silbergelatinedruck
Rayographe (spirales de pellicule), épreuve gélatino-
argentique
Rayograph (spiralen van filmstrips), gelatinezilverdruk
1923
29,4 x 23,5 cm / 11.5 x 9.25 in.
Museum of Modern Art, New York

▶ **Man Ray**
(Philadelphia 1890 - Paris 1976)
Rayograph (Clock Wheels), gelatin silver print
Fotogramm (Zahnräder einer Uhr), Silbergelatinedruck
Rayographe (rouages d'horloge), épreuve gélatino-argentique
Rayograph (raderen van een klok - Clock Wheels),
gelatinezilverdruk
1925
28,3 x 22,9 cm / 11.1 x 9 in.
Yale University Art Gallery, New Haven

Yves Tanguy
(Paris 1900 - Woodbury, CT. 1955)
The extinction of useless lights, oil on canvas
Ausschalten unnötiger Lichter, Öl auf Leinwand
Extinction des lumières inutiles, huile sur toile
Het doven van onnodige lichten, olieverf op doek
1927
92,1 x 65,4 cm / 36.2 x 25.7 in.
Museum of Modern Art, New York

Yves Tanguy
(Paris 1900 - Woodbury, CT. 1955)
Parallels, oil on canvas
Die Parallelen, Öl auf Leinwand
Les Parallèles, huile sur toile
De Parallellen, olieverf op doek
1929
92,2 x 73 cm / 36.2 x 28.7 in.
Philadelphia Museum of Art, Philadelphia

Yves Tanguy
(Paris 1900 - Woodbury, CT.
1955)
Untitled, decalcomania (ink
transfer) on paper
Ohne Titel, Tintenabziehbild auf
Papier
Sans titre, décalcomanie et
encre sur papier
Zonder titel, decalcomanie, inkt
op papier
1936
32,5 x 50,2 cm / 12.7 x 19.7 in.
Private Collection /
Privatsammlung / Collection
privée / Privécollectie

Yves Tanguy
(Paris 1900 - Woodbury, CT. 1955)
Slowly towards the north, oil on canvas
Langsam nach Norden, Öl auf Leinwand
Vers le nord lentement, huile sur toile
Langzaam naar het noorden, olieverf op doek
1942
106,7 x 91,4 cm / 42 x 35.9 in.
Museum of Modern Art, New York

▶ **André Masson**
(Balagny-sur-Thérain 1896 - Paris 1987)
Cabaret, oil on canvas
Im Cabaret, Öl auf Leinwand
Au cabaret, huile sur toile
Bij het cabaret, olieverf op doek
1923
41 x 27 cm / 16.1 x 10.6 in.
Private Collection / Privatsammlung / Collection privée / Privécollectie

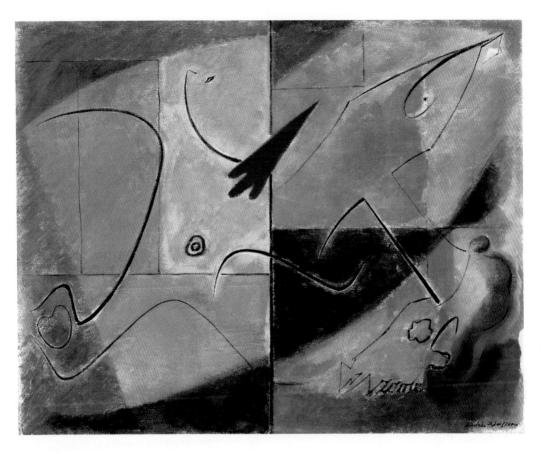

André Masson
(Balagny-sur-Thérain 1896 - Paris 1987)
Butcher, oil on canvas
Der Metzger, Öl auf Leinwand
Le Boucher, huile sur toile
De slager, olieverf op doek
1928
73,5 x 92,5 cm / 28.9 x 36.4 in.
Hamburger Kunsthalle, Hamburg

◀ **André Masson**
(Balagny-sur-Thérain 1896 - Paris 1987)
Wing, oil on canvas
Der Flügel, Öl auf Leinwand
L'Aile, huile sur toile
De vleugel, olieverf op doek
1925
55 x 36 cm / 21.6 x 14.1 in.
Nationalgalerie, Museum Berggruen, Staatliche Museen zu Berlin, Berlin

❚ *"To live and to stop living are imaginary solutions. Existence is elsewhere."*
❚ *"Leben und aufhören zu leben sind imaginäre Lösungen. Die Existenz ist anderswo."*
❚ *« Vivre et cesser de vivre sont des solutions imaginaires. L'existence est ailleurs. »*
❚ *"Leven en ophouden te leven zijn denkbeeldige oplossingen. Het bestaan is elders."*
André Breton

André Masson
(Balagny-sur-Thérain 1896 - Paris 1987)
Labyrinth, oil on canvas
Das Labyrinth, Öl auf Leinwand
Le Labyrinthe, huile sur toile
Het labyrint, olieverf op doek
1938
130,5 x 106,5 cm / 51.3 x 41.9 in.
Centre Georges Pompidou, Musée National d'Art Moderne, Paris

◀ **André Masson**
(Balagny-sur-Thérain 1896 - Paris 1987)
Blue self-portrait, mixed technique on paper
Selbsbildnis in Blau, Mischtechnik auf Papier
Autoportrait en bleu, technique mixte sur papier
Zelfportret in blauw, gemengde techniek op papier
1934
51 x 34 cm / 20 x 13.3 in.
Private Collection / Privatsammlung / Collection privée / Privécollectie

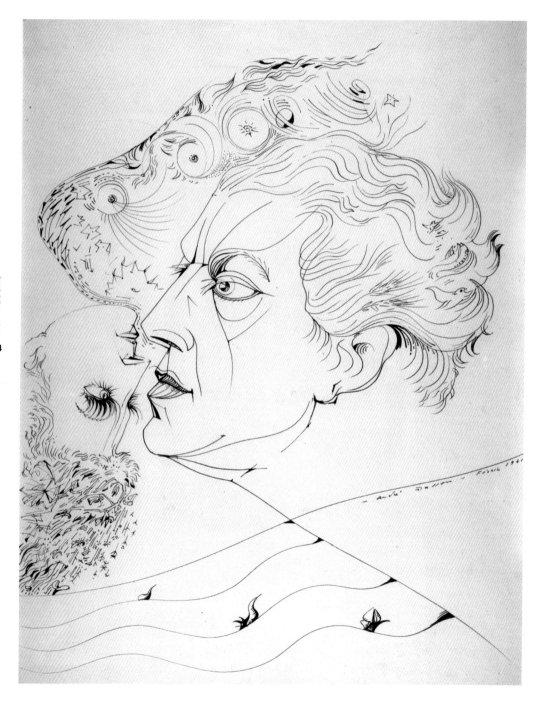

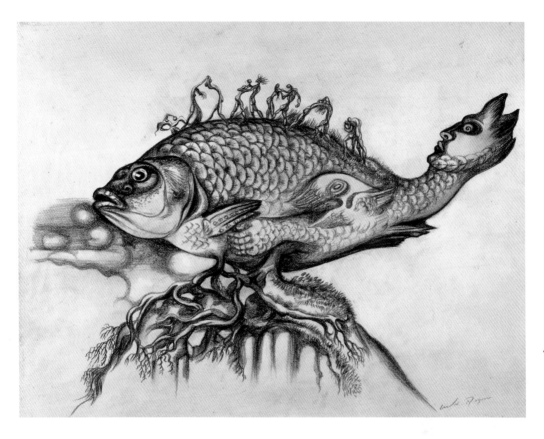

André Masson
(Balagny-sur-Thérain 1896 - Paris 1987)
Armida's garden, pastel on paper
Der Garten von Armida, Pastell auf papier
Le Jardin d'Armide, Pastel sur Papier
De tuin van Armida, pastel op papier
1940
47,5 x 62,5 cm / 18.7 x 24.6 in.
Private Collection / Privatsammlung / Collection privée / Privécollectie

◀ **André Masson**
(Balagny-sur-Thérain 1896 - Paris 1987)
Portrait of Jacqueline Lamba and André Breton, ink on canvas
Porträt von Jacqueline Lamba und André Breton, Tinte auf Leinwand
Portraits de Jacqueline Lamba et André Breton, encre sur toile
Portret van Jacqueline Lamba en André Breton, inkt op doek
1940
60 x 47 cm / 23.6 x 18.5 in.
Private Collection / Privatsammlung / Collection privée / Privécollectie

André Masson
(Balagny-sur-Thérain 1896 - Paris 1987)
For the journey, mixed technique on paper
Für die Reise, Mischtechnik auf Papier
Pour le voyage, technique mixte sur papier
Voor de reis, gemengde techniek op papier
1941
37,7 x 27 cm / 14.8 x 10.6 in.
Private Collection / Privatsammlung /
Collection privée / Privécollectie

▌ *"Get rid of your wife. Get rid of your lover. Get rid of your hopes and fears. Abandon your children in the open country-side. Leave certainty and uncertainty. Take to the road!"*
▌ *"Lasst eure Frau. Lasst eure Geliebte. Lasst Hoffnungen und Ängste. Entledigt euch eurer Kindern auf freiem Feld. Lasst die Sicherheit für die Unsicherheit. Macht euch auf den Weg!"*
▌ *« Lâchez votre femme. Lâchez votre amant. Lâchez vos espérances et vos craintes. Débarrassez-vous des enfants en pleine campagne. Laissez le certain pour l'incertain. Partez sur les routes! »*
▌ *"Verlaat je vrouw. Verlaat je minnares. Verlaat je hoop en angsten. Laat je kinderen achter in het bos. Laat het zekere voor het onzekere. Vertrek en ga op weg!"*
André Breton

André Masson
(Balagny-sur-Thérain 1896 - Paris 1987)
Landscape in the shape of a fish, oil on canvas
Landschaft in Form eines Fisches, Öl auf Leinwand
Paysage en forme de poisson, huile sur toile
Landschap in de vorm van vissen, olieverf op doek
1941
31,1 x 46,1 cm / 12.2 x 18.1 in.
Private Collection / Privatsammlung /
Collection privée / Privécollectie

▌ *"Surrealism: the pure psychic automatism with which we attempt to express ourselves, either verbally, or written, or in some other way, is the real function of thought."*
▌ *"Surrealismus: reiner psychischer Automatismus, mit dem man sich vornimmt, das reale Funktionieren des Gedankens wörtlich, schriftlich oder auf anderem Weg auszudrücken."*
▌ *« Surréalisme : automatisme psychique pur par lequel on se propose d'exprimer, soit verbalement, soit par écrit, soit de tout autre manière, le fonctionnement réel de la pensée. »*
▌ *"Surrealisme: Puur psychisch automatisme waarmee men zich voorneemt om, in woord en geschrift of op welke andere manier ook, de wezenlijke werking van het denken tot uitdrukking te brengen."*
André Breton

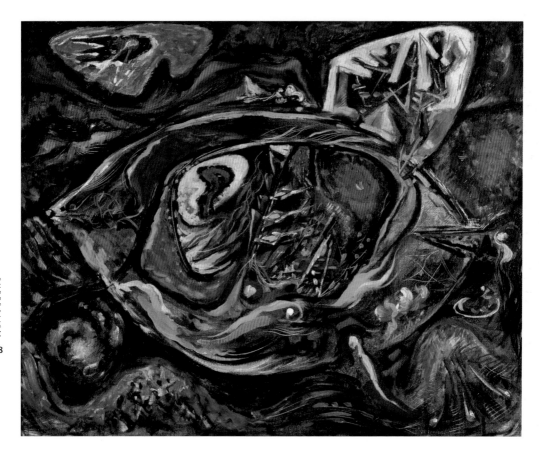

André Masson
(Balagny-sur-Thérain 1896 - Paris 1987)
Germination, oil on canvas
Keimung, Öl auf Leinwand
Germination, huile sur toile
Ontkieming (Germination), olieverf op doek
1942
50 x 63 cm / 19.2 x 24.8 in.
Private Collection / Privatsammlung / Collection privée / Privécollectie

André Masson
(Balagny-sur-Thérain 1896 - Paris 1987)
Birth of a bird, watercolour and pastel on paper
Die Geburt eines Vogels, Aquarell und Pastell auf Papier
Naissance d'un oiseau, aquarelle et pastel sur papier
Geboorte van een vogel (Naissance d'un oiseau), aquarel en pastel op papier
1942
60,5 x 70,5 cm / 23.8 x 27.7 in.
Private Collection / Privatsammlung / Collection privée / Privécollectie

Roberto Sebastian Matta
(Santiago de Chile 1911 - Civitavecchia 2002)
The Fabulous Race-Track of Death (Instrument Very Dangerous to the Eye), oil on canvas
Fantastisches Rennen des Todes (Gegenstand sehr gefährlich für die Augen), Öl auf Leinwand
Course fantastique de la mort (instrument très dangereux pour les yeux), huile sur toile
Fantastisch dodelijke renbaan (zeer gevaarlijk instrument voor de ogen), olieverf op doek
1941
71,1 x 91,4 cm / 27.9 x 35.9 in.
Yale University Art Gallery, New Haven

Roberto Sebastian Matta
(Santiago de Chile 1911 - Civitavecchia 2002)
The vertigo of Eros, oil on canvas
Der Schwindel von Eros, Öl auf Leinwand
Le Vertige d'Éros, huile sur toile
De vertigo van Eros, olieverf op doek
1944
195,6 x 251,5 cm / 77 x 99 in.
Museum of Modern Art, New York

Francis Picabia
(Paris 1879 - 1953)
The sphinx, oil on canvas
Die Sphynx, Öl auf Leinwand
Sphinx, huile sur toile
De sfinx, olieverf op doek
1929
131 x 163 cm / 51.5 x 64.1 in.
Centre Georges Pompidou, Musée National d'Art Moderne, Paris

◀ **Francis Picabia**
(Paris 1879 - 1953)
Optophone II
Oil on canvas
Öl auf Leinwand
Huile sur toile
Olieverf op doek
1922-1924
116 x 88 cm / 45.6 x 34.6 in.
Centre Georges Pompidou, Musée National d'Art Moderne, Paris

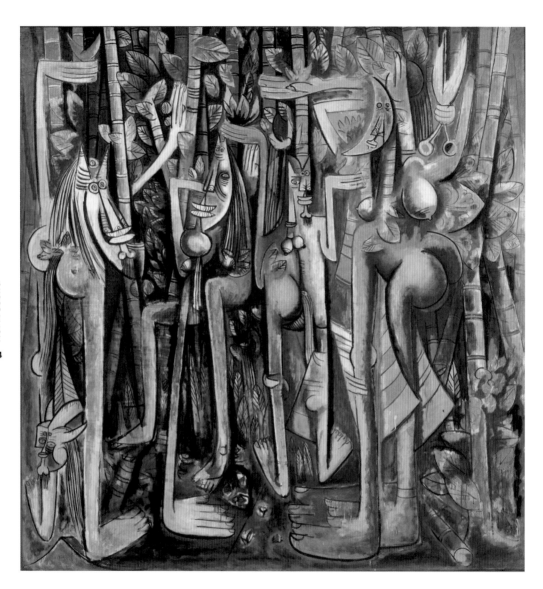

Wifredo Lam
(Sagua la Grande, Cuba 1902 - Paris 1982)
The jungle, gouache on paper mounted on canvas
Der Dschungel, Gouache auf Papier aufgetragen auf Leinwand
La jungle, gouache sur papier, marouflé sur toile
De jungle, gouache op papier op doek
1943
239,4 x 229,9 cm / 94.2 x 90.5 in.
Museum of Modern Art, New York

Wifredo Lam
(Sagua la Grande, Cuba 1902 - Paris 1982)
Untitled, ink on paper
Ohne Titel, Tinte auf Papier
Sans titre, encre sur papier
Zonder titel, inkt op papier
1946
31 x 24 cm / 12.2 x 9.4 in.
Private Collection / Privatsammlung / Collection privée / Privécollectie

ces terrains vagues et la lune

accrochée à la maison de mon coeur

vaincu par l'ombre

où j'erre

André Breton
(Tinchebray 1896 - Paris 1966)
Poesie-Objet, assemblage mounted on wood
Gedicht-Objekt, Assemblage auf Holz
Poème-Objet, assemblage monté sur bois
Poëzie-object, assemblage op hout
1941
45,8 x 53,2 x 10,9 cm / 18 x 20.9 x 4.2 in.
Museum of Modern Art, New York

Marcel Duchamp
(Blainville 1887 - Neuilly-sur-Seine 1968)
Boîte-en-valise, assemblage: suitcase in brown leather with a handle containing 69 miniature
objects and prints and one original, virgin (no. 2), coloured collotype
Schachtel im Koffer, Assemblage: brauner Lederkoffer mit Griff, der 69 Miniaturreplikate,
Druckreplikate und ein Original beinhaltet, Jungfrau (Nr.2), farbiger Lichtdruck.
Boîte en valise, assemblage : valise en peau marron avec poignée, contenant 69 répliques en
miniature et reproductions gravées, et un original, virgin (boîte n.2), collotype colorié
De doos in de koffer, assemblage: bruinleren koffer met handvat, met 69 miniatuur replica's,
reproducties en een origineel schilderij maagd (nr. 2) lichtdruk in kleur
1938
Philadelphia Museum of Art, Philadelphia

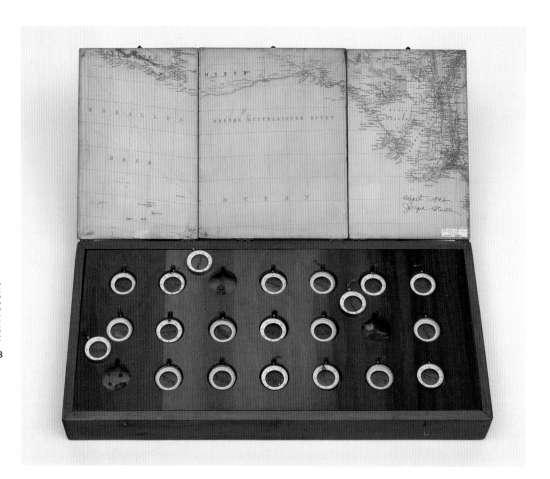

Joseph Cornell
(Nyack, New York 1903 - New York 1972)
Object (Rose wind), assemblage: wooden box with various objects
Objekt (Windrosen), Assemblage in Holzschachtel mit verschiedenen Gegenständen
Objet (Rose des vents), assemblage : boîte en bois divisée en dix-sept compartiments et
contenant un mélange d'objets, servant de support à l'œuvre précédente
Object (Windroos), assemblage in kist met diverse voorwerpen
1943-1953
6,7 x 53,7 x 26,2 cm / 2.6 x 21.1 x 10.3 in.
Museum of Modern Art, New York

Joseph Cornell
(Nyack, New York 1903 - New York 1972)
Object (Rose wind), assemblage: wooden box with 17 compartments containing miscellaneous objects
Objekt (Windrosen), Assemblage: Holzschachtel geteilt in 17 Fächer die verschiedene Gegenstände beinhalten
Objet (Rose des vents), assemblage : boîte en bois comportant vingt et une boussoles
Object (Windroos), assemblage: kist verdeeld in 17 compartimenten met verschillende voorwerpen
1943-1953
6,7 x 53,7 x 26,2 cm / 2.6 x 21.1 x 10.3 in.
Museum of Modern Art, New York

This is the colour of my dreams

At once abstract and representational, Surrealist canvases were animated by objects of various shapes and kind depicted in gaudy colours distributed across the canvas in vivid and playful sequence. Movement and stillness, chromatic energy and fantastic forms, these are the central themes of Surrealist art, in its untiring exploration of the evocative power of dreams.

Dies ist die Farbe meiner Träume

Im perfekten Gleichgewicht zwischen Figur und Abstraktion wuchern im Raum Objekte verschiedener Form und Natur, deren Ausdruck durch schreiende Farben unterstrichen wird, während sich die Leinwand mit leuchtenden, lebhaften und spielerischen Kolorierungen vollsaugt. Bewegung und Stillstand, Farbenergie und phantastische Formen: das ist die Sprache, die das Universum des Surrealen zusammensetzt und dabei direkt auf die Beschwörungsmacht der Träume zurückgreift.

Ceci est la couleur de mes rêves

En parfait équilibre entre figuration et abstraction naît un espace foisonnant d'objets de forme et de nature variées, dont l'aspect est rehaussé par l'éclat tapageur de la palette, tandis que la toile se couvre de couleurs brillantes, vives et joyeuses. Mouvement et repos, énergie chromatique et formes fantastiques : tels sont les concepts qui composent l'univers protéiforme de la surréalité, en participant directement de la puissance évocatrice des rêves.

Dit is de kleur van mijn dromen

Bij een perfect evenwicht tussen figuratie en abstractie, ontstaat een prolifererende ruimte van voorwerpen van verschillende vorm en aard, wiens aspecten worden geprezen met een opvallend palet, terwijl het doek wordt doordrenkt met schitterende, levendige en speelse tinten. Beweging en stilstand, chromatische energie en fantasievormen: dit zijn de woorden die horen bij de wereld van de surrealiteit, direct afgeleid van de evocatieve kracht van dromen.

2

Forms and colours in Surrealism
Formen und Farben des Surrealismus
Formes et couleurs du Surréalisme
Vormen en kleuren van het Surrealisme

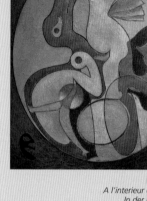

Joan Miró
Dog barking at the moon
Hund, den Mond anbellend
Chien aboyant à la lune
Hond naar de maan blaffend
1926
Philadelphia Museum of Art,
Philadelphia

Max Ernst
A l'interieur de la Vue
In der Übersicht
À l'intérieur de la vue
Het binnenste van het Zien
1929
Centre Georges Pompidou, Musée
National d'Art Moderne, Paris

1926   1928   1930   1932

Alberto Savinio
The graces of the island
Die Grazien der Insel
L'île des charmes charmes de l'île
De gratiën van het eiland
1928
Private Collection / Privatsammlung /
Collection privée / Privécollectie

René Magritte
La voix des airs
Die Stimme der Luft
La Voix de l'air
De stem van de ruimte
1931
Collezione Peggy
Guggenheim, Venezia

Balthus
The street
Die Straße
La Rue
De straat
1933
Museum of Modern Art, New York

Pablo Picasso
Seated woman with a book
Sitzende Frau mit einem Buch
Femme assise avec livre
Zittende vrouw met een boek
1937
Private Collection / Privatsammlung /
Collection privée / Privécollectie

1934   **1936**   **1938**   **1940**

Salvador Dalí
Untitled (small theatre)
Ohne Titel (kleines Theater)
Sans titre (Petit théâtre)
Zonder titel (Klein theater) Museum of
1934
Museum of Modern Art, New York

Hans Bellmer
Portrait of Joe Bousquet
Porträt des Joe Bousquet
Portrait de Joë Bousquet
Portret van Joe Bousquet
1940
Musée Cantini, Marseille

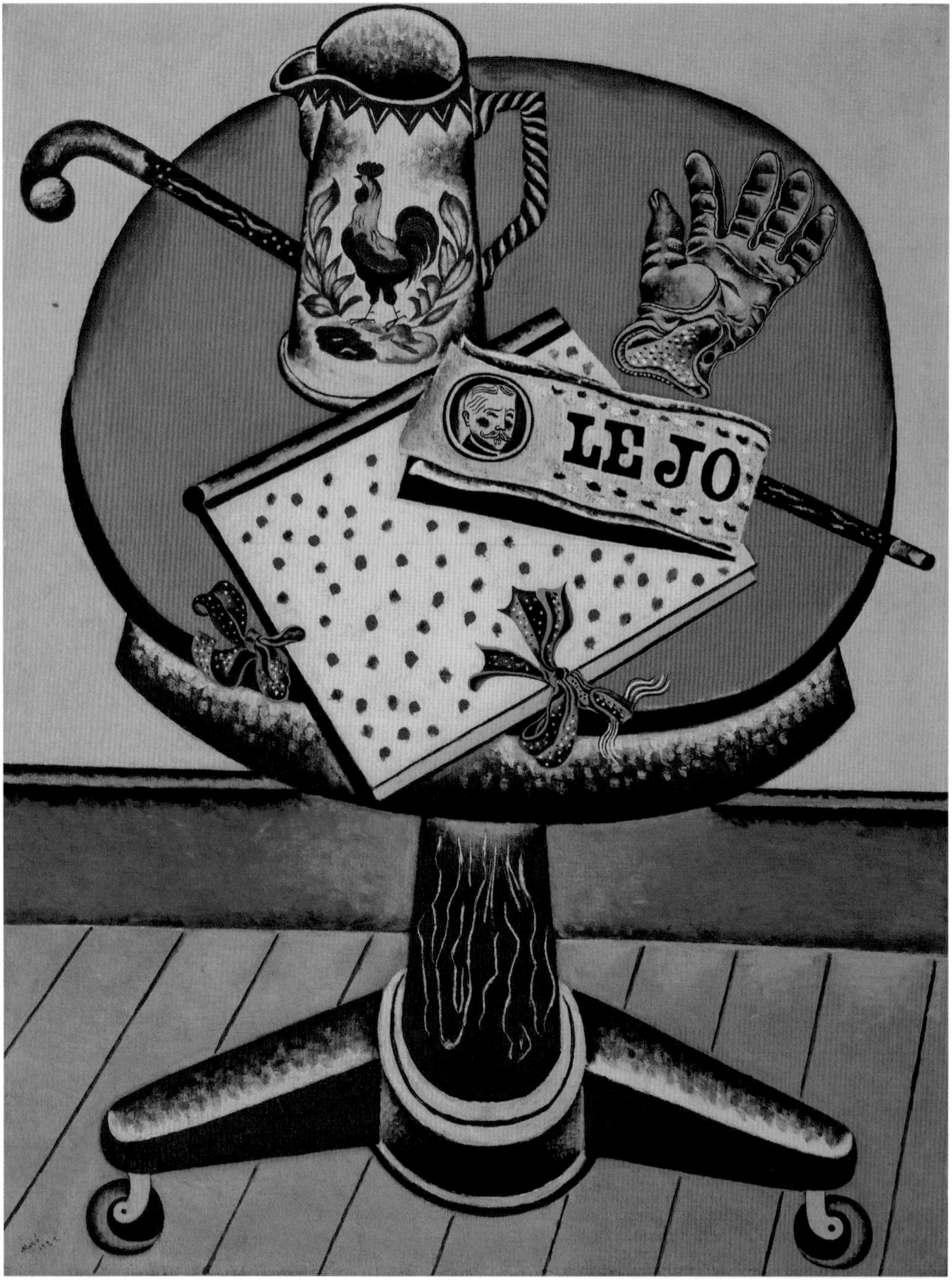
LE JO

Joan Miró
(Barcelona 1893 - Palma de Mallorca 1983)
Catalan landscape (The Hunter), oil on canvas
Der Jäger (Katalanische Landschaft), Öl auf Leinwand
Le Chasseur (Paysage catalan), huile sur toile
De jager (Catalaans landschap), olieverf op doek
1923-1924
64,8 x 100,3 cm / 25.5 x 39.4 in.
Museum of Modern Art, New York

◀ **Joan Miró**
(Barcelona 1893 - Palma de Mallorca 1983)
Still life - Glove and newspaper, oil on canvas
Stillleben - Handschuh und Zeitung, Öl auf Leinwand
Nature morte - Gant et journal, huile sur toile
Stilleven - Handschoen en krant, olieverf op doek
1921
46 x 35 cm / 18.1 x 13.7 in.
Museum of Modern Art, New York

Joan Miró
(Barcelona 1893 - Palma de Mallorca 1983)
Animated landscape, oil on canvas
Belebte Landschaft, Öl auf Leinwand
Paysage animé, huile sur toile
Bezield landschap (Animated landscape), olieverf op doek
1927
129,5 x 195 cm / 50.9 x 76.7 in.
Metropolitan Museum of Art, New York

▶ **Joan Miró**
(Barcelona 1893 - Palma de Mallorca 1983)
The potato, oil on canvas
Die Kartoffel, Öl auf Leinwand
La Patate, huile sur toile
De aardappel, olieverf op doek
1928
101 x 81,6 cm / 39.7 x 32.1 in.
Metropolitan Museum of Art, New York

Joan Miró
(Barcelona 1893 - Palma de Mallorca 1983)
Dutch interior, oil on canvas
Holländisches Innere, Öl auf Leinwand
Intérieur hollandais, huile sur toile
Hollands interieur, olieverf op doek
1928
129,9 x 96,8 cm / 51.1 x 38.1 in.
Metropolitan Museum of Art, New York

▶ **Joan Miró**
(Barcelona 1893 - Palma de Mallorca 1983)
Dutch interior, oil on canvas
Holländisches Innere, Öl auf Leinwand
Intérieur hollandais, huile sur toile
Hollands interieur, olieverf op doek
1928
91,8 x 73 cm / 36.1 x 28.7 in.
Museum of Modern Art, New York

Joan Miró
(Barcelona 1893 - Palma de Mallorca 1983)
Painting, oil, pencil and paper on a sheet of sand paper
Bild, Öl, Lapiz und Papier auf Schleifpapier
Peinture, huile, lapis et papier sur feuille de papier émeri
Schilderij, olieverf, grafiet en papier op schuurpapier
1934
36,2 x 23,5 cm / 14.2 x 9.2 in.
Philadelphia Museum of Art, Philadelphia

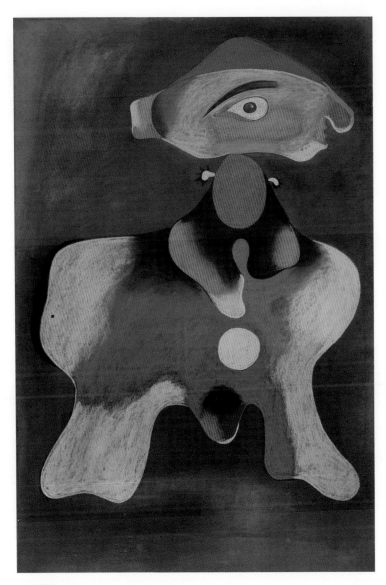

Joan Miró
(Barcelona 1893 - Palma de Mallorca 1983)
Woman, pastel and grafite on paper prepared by the artist with sand and glue
Frau, Pastell und Bleistift auf vom Künstler mit Sand und Leim präpariertem Papier
Femme, pastel et mine de plomb, sur papier préparé par l'artiste avec du sable et de la colle
Vrouw, pastel en grafiet op papier, geprepareerd door de kunstenaar met zand en lijm
1934
107 x 71,4 cm / 42.1 x 28.1 in.
Philadelphia Museum of Art, Philadelphia

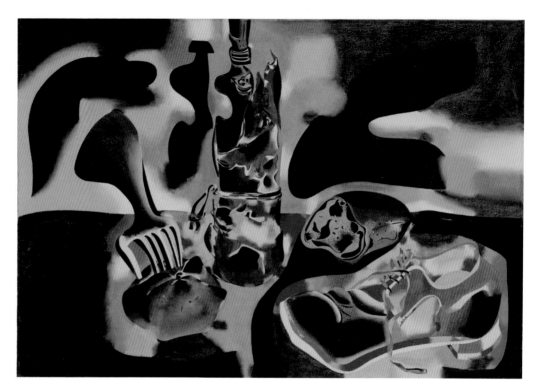

▌ "I work like a gardener or a winemaker. Things mature slowly. I didn't discover my vocabulary of form in a flash. It developed almost despite myself."
▌ "Ich arbeite wie ein Gärtner oder wie ein Winzer. Die Dinge reifen langsam. Meinen Wortschatz an Formen habe ich nicht auf einen Schlag entdeckt. Er hat sich fast gegen meinen Willen geformt."
▌ « Je travaille comme un jardinier ou comme un vigneron. Les choses mûrissent lentement. Mon vocabulaire de formes, je ne l'ai pas découvert d'un seul coup ; il s'est formé presque malgré moi. »
▌ "Ik werk als een tuinman of als een wijnbouwer. De dingen groeien langzaam. Mijn vormentaal ontdek ik niet plotseling. Die ontstaat bijna vanzelf."
Joan Miró

Joan Miró
(Barcelona 1893 - Palma de Mallorca 1983)
Still life with an old shoe, oil on canvas
Stillleben mit altem Schuh, Öl auf Leinwand
Nature morte et vieille chaussure, huile sur toile
Stilleven met oude schoen, olieverf op doek
1937
81,3 x 116,8 cm / 32 x 45.9 in.
Museum of Modern Art, New York

Joan Miró
(Barcelona 1893 - Palma de Mallorca 1983)
Constellation: women on the beach, gouache and oil on paper
Konstellation: Frauen am Strand, Gouache und Öl auf Papier
Constellation : femmes sur la plage, gouache et huile sur papier
Constellatie: vrouwen aan het strand, gouache en olieverf op papier
1940
Metropolitan Museum of Art, New York

▌ "Immobile things become magnificent. Much more magnificent than those in movement."
▌ "Die unbeweglichen Dinge werden großartig. Viel großartiger als die beweglichen."
▌ « Les choses immobiles deviennent grandioses. Bien plus grandioses que celles en mouvement. »
▌ "De onbeweeglijke dingen worden groots. Veel groter dan de beweeglijke."
Joan Miró

Joan Miró
(Barcelona 1893 - Palma de Mallorca 1983)
Women and birds in the night, gouache on canvas
Frauen und Vögel in der Nacht, Gouache auf Leinwand
Femmes et oiseaux dans la nuit, gouache sur toile
Vrouwen en vogels in de nacht, gouache op doek
1944
23,5 x 42 cm / 9.2 x 16.5 in.
Metropolitan Museum of Art, New York

◀ **Joan Miró**
(Barcelona 1893 - Palma de Mallorca 1983)
Constellation: awakening at dawn, gouache and oil patina on paper
Konstellation: Erwachen im Morgengrauen, Gouache und Ölfilm auf Papier
Constellation : réveil au petit jour, gouache et patine d'huile sur papier
Constellatie: ontwaken in de vroege ochtend, gouache en oliepatina op papier
1941
46,0 x 38,0 cm / 18.1 x 14.9 in.
Kimbell Art Museum, Fort Worth

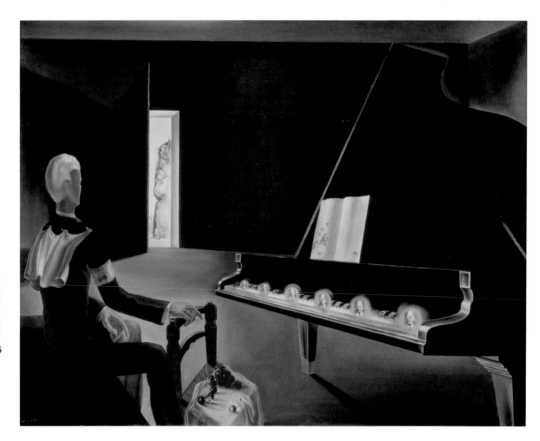

Salvador Dalí
(Figueres 1904 - 1989)
Partial hallucination: six apparitions of Lenin on a Grand Piano, oil on canvas
Partielle Sinnestäuschung: Sechs Erscheinungen Lenins auf dem Flügel, Öl auf Leinwand
Hallucination partielle : six images de Lénine sur un piano, huile et vernis sur toile
Gedeeltelijke hallucinatie: zes verschijningen van Lenin op een pianovleugel, olieverf op doek
1931
114 x 146 cm / 44.8 x 57.4 in.
Centre Georges Pompidou, Musée National d'Art Moderne, Paris

▶ **Salvador Dalí**
(Figueres 1904 - 1989)
The birth of liquid anxieties, oil on canvas
Die Geburt der flüssigen Ängste, Öl auf Leinwand
Naissance de l'anxiété liquide, huile sur toile
De geboorte van de vloeibare angsten, olieverf op doek
1932
86,5 x 70 cm / 34 x 27.5 in.
Hamburger Kunsthalle, Hamburg

■ *"There are irrational and unspeakable acts of violence that periodically illuminate the desolate moral panorama."*
■ *"Es gibt Gewaltakte, unqualifizierbare und irrationale, die mit ihrem beispielhaften Licht immer wieder das desolate moralische Panorama beleuchten."*
■ *« Il y a des actes de violence inqualifiables et irrationnels qui illuminent périodiquement de leur éclat exemplaire un panorama moral dévasté. »*
■ *"Er zijn daden van geweld, verachtelijk en irrationeel, die steeds weer het verwaarloosde morele panorama verlichten, met hun verblindende voorbeeld."*
Salvador Dalí

Salvador Dalí
(Figueres 1904 - 1989)
The phantom Cart, oil on wood
Der Geisterwagen, Öl auf Holz
Le Chariot fantôme, huile sur bois
De spookwagen, olieverf op hout
1933
15,9 x 21,9 cm / 6.2 x 8.6 in.
Yale University Art Gallery, New Haven

▌ *"Abstract art collapses in front of us never to rise again after having seen the eye of a girl slashed by a razor blade."*
▌ *"Die abstrakte Kunst fiel vor uns nieder, um sich nie wieder zu erheben, nachdem sie das mit einer Rasierklinge durchschnittene Auge eines Mädchens gesehen hatte."*
▌ *« L'art abstrait nous est tombé dessus sans plus jamais se relever, après avoir vu un œil de jeune fille découpé par une lame de rasoir. »*
▌ *"De abstracte kunst viel voor ons neer om vervolgens nooit meer op te staan, nadat ze het opensnijden van het oog van een meisje met een scheermes had aanschouwd."*
Salvador Dalí

Salvador Dalí
(Figueres 1904 - 1989)
Untitled (small theatre), wood and painted glass
Ohne Titel (kleines Theater), bemaltes Holz und Glas
Sans titre (Petit théâtre), bois et verre peint
Zonder titel (Klein theater), hout en beschilderd glas
1934
32,3 x 42,5 x 31,1 cm / 12.7 x 16.7 x 12.2 in.
Museum of Modern Art, New York

Salvador Dalí
(Figueres 1904 -1989)
Soft construction with boiled beans (Premonition of the Civil War), oil on canvas
Weiche Konstruktion mit gekochten Bohnen, Öl auf Leinwand
Construction molle avec haricots bouillis (Prémonition de la guerre civile), huile sur toile
Weke constructie met gekookte bonen (Voorgevoel van de Burgeroorlog), olieverf op doek
1936
99,9 x 100 cm / 39.3 x 39.3 in.
Philadelphia Museum of Art, The Louise and Walter Arensberg Collection, Philadelphia

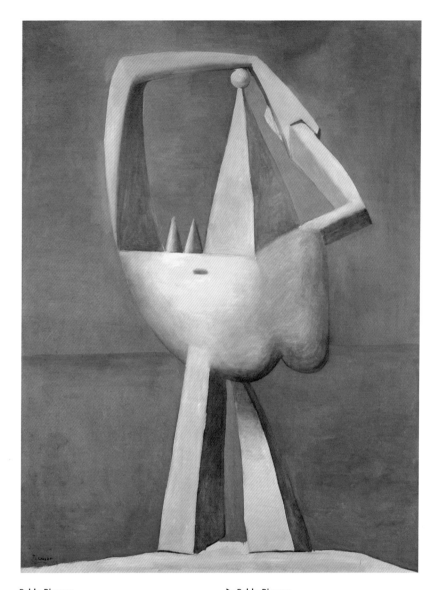

Pablo Picasso
(Málaga 1881 - Mougins 1973)
Nude, oil on canvas
Nackte am Meer, Öl auf Leinwand
Nu au bord de la mer, huile sur toile
Staand naakt aan zee, olieverf op doek
1929
129,9 x 96,8 cm / 51.1 x 38.1 in.
Metropolitan Museum of Art, New York

▶ **Pablo Picasso**
(Málaga 1881 - Mougins 1973)
Seated bather, oil on canvas
Sitzende Frau am Meeresufer, Öl auf Leinwand
Baigneuse assise, huile sur toile
Zittende baadster, olieverf op doek
1930
163,2 x 129,5 cm / 64.2 x 50.9 in.
Museum of Modern Art, New York

Pablo Picasso
(Málaga 1881 - Mougins 1973)
Women playing on the beach, oil, pastel and pencil on paper
Spielende Frauen am Strand, Öl, Pastell und Bleistift auf Leinwand
Femmes jouant sur la plage, huile, pastel et mine de plomb sur toile
Op het strand, olieverf, pastel en potlood op doek
1937
129 x 194 cm / 50.7 x 76.3 in.
Collezione Peggy Guggenheim, Venezia

◀ **Pablo Picasso**
(Málaga 1881 - Mougins 1973)
Seated woman with a book, oil on canvas
Sitzende Frau mit einem Buch, Öl auf Leinwand
Femme assise avec livre, huile sur toile
Zittende vrouw met een boek, olieverf op doek
1937
92 x 65 cm / 36.2 x 25.5 in.
Private Collection / Privatsammlung / Collection privée / Privécollectie

▌ *"Don't resist the thread of your destiny that colours the crystal with mud, extenuating the gold locked in memories burnt on a grill of azure and mint."*
▌ *"Keinen Wiederstand leisten dem Faden, der das Schicksal spinnt, der den Diebstahl von Kristall mit Schlamm färbt, der an der Stunde der Erinnerungen zehrt, die auf einem blauen und minzfarbenen Grill verbrennen."*
▌ *« Ne pas s'opposer au fil que travaille le destin que barbouille le vol de cristal de boue qu'épuise l'heure enveloppée dans des souvenirs brûlés sur une grille de bleu et de menthe. »*
▌ *"Biedt geen weerstand tegen het draad dat het lot uitvoert, die de diefstal van het kristal met modder kleurt, dat teert op het uur opgenomen in de herinneringen verbrand op een blauw- en mintkleurig rooster."*
Pablo Picasso

Max Ernst
(Brühl 1891 - Paris 1976)
Le repos du mort
Pencil on paper
Bleistift auf Papier
Mine de plomb sur papier
Potlood op papier
1925
30 x 41 cm / 11.8 x 16.1 in.
Private Collection / Privatsammlung / Collection privée / Privécollectie

▶ **Max Ernst**
(Brühl 1891 - Paris 1976)
L'oiseau forestier, oil on canvas
Der Waldvogel, Öl auf Leinwand
L'Oiseau forestier, huile sur toile
De bosvogel, olieverf op doek
1927
31 x 22 cm / 12.2 x 8.6 in.
Musée Picasso, Paris

Max Ernst
(Brühl 1891 - Paris 1976)
The barbarians, oil on paper and board mounted on a wooden frame
Die Barbaren, Öl auf Papier und Karton aufgetragen auf Holzrahmen
Les Barbares, huile sur papier et carton, montés sur un châssis de bois
De barbaren, olieverf op papier en karton op houten frame
1937
24,1 x 24,1 cm / 9.4 x 9.4 in.
Private Collection / Privatsammlung / Collection privée / Privécollectie

Max Ernst
(Brühl 1891 - Paris 1976)
The barbarians, oil on board
Die Barbaren, Öl auf Karton
Les Barbares, huile sur carton
De barbaren, Olieverf op karton
1937
24 x 33 cm / 9.4 x 12.9 in.
Metropolitan Museum of Art, New York

Max Ernst
(Brühl 1891 - Paris 1976)
Napoleon in the desert, oil on canvas
Napoleon in der Wildnis, Öl auf Leinwand
Napoléon dans le désert, huile sur toile
Napoleon in de wildernis, olieverf op doek
1941
46,3 x 38,1 cm / 18.2 x 14.9 in.
Museum of Modern Art, New York

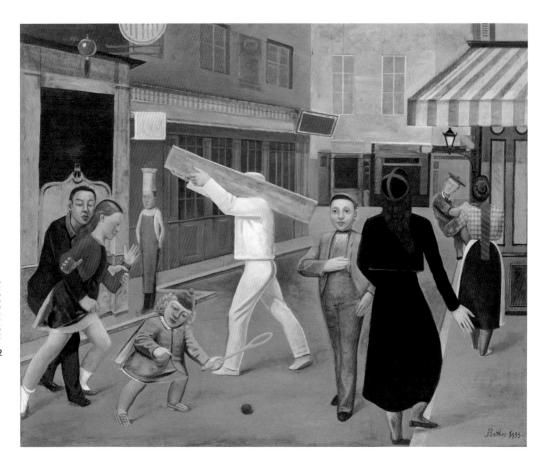

Balthus
(Paris 1908 - Rossinière 2001)
The street, oil on canvas
Die Straße, Öl auf Leinwand
La Rue, huile sur toile
De straat, olieverf op doek
1933
195 x 240 cm / 76.7 x 94.4 in.
Museum of Modern Art, New York

Balthus
(Paris 1908 - Rossinière 2001)
The mountain, oil on canvas
Der Berg, Öl auf Leinwand
La Montagne, huile sur toile
De berg, olieverf op doek
1937
248,9 x 365,8 cm / 97.9 x 144 in.
Metropolitan Museum of Art, New York

▌ *"It happens that I remember things dreamed of at night. Their recall brings great happiness. It's like a victory for me when I manage to recover the world of my dreams."*

▌ *"Es geschieht, dass ich mich der nächtlichen Träume erinnere. Ich erinnre mich ihrer mit großer Freude. Es ist wie ein Sieg für mich, wenn es mir gelingt, meine Traumwelt wiederzuerlangen."*

▌ *« Il arrive que je me souvienne des choses rêvées la nuit. Je me les rappelle avec un grand bonheur. C'est une victoire pour moi quand je réussis à récupérer le monde de mes rêves. »*

▌ *"Het komt voor dat ik mij mijn nachtelijke dromen herinner. Ik herinner ze mij met grote vreugde. Het is als een overwinning voor mij, wanneer het mij lukt mijn droomwereld terug te halen."*
René Magritte

René Magritte
(Lessen 1898 - Brussel 1967)
The scent of the abyss, oil on canvas
Der Duft des Abgrunds, Öl auf Leinwand
Le Parfum de l'abîme, huile sur toile
De geur van het ravijn, olieverf op doek
1928
54 x 73 cm / 21.2 x 28.7 in.
Private Collection / Privatsammlung / Collection privée / Privécollectie

René Magritte
(Lessen 1898 - Brussel 1967)
Familiar objects, oil on canvas
Die Erbstücke, Öl auf Leinwand
Les Objets familiers, huile sur toile
De familievoorwerpen, olieverf op doek
1928
81 x 116 cm / 31.8 x 45.6 in.
Private Collection / Privatsammlung / Collection privée / Privécollectie

René Magritte
(Lessen 1898 - Brussel 1967)
The Heart of the Matter, oil on canvas
Der Kern der Geschichte, Öl auf Leinwand
L'Histoire centrale, huile sur toile
Het hart van de zaak, olieverf op doek
1928
116 x 81 cm / 45.6 x 31.8 in.
Private Collection / Privatsammlung / Collection privée / Privécollectie

René Magritte
(Lessen 1898 - Brussel 1967)
La voix des airs, oil on canvas
Die Stimme der Luft, Öl auf Leinwand
La Voix de l'air, huile sur toile
De stem van de ruimte, olieverf op doek
1931
73 x 54 cm / 28.7 x 21.2 in.
Collezione Peggy Guggenheim, Venezia

René Magritte
(Lessen 1898 - Brussel 1967)
Le retour, oil on canvas
Der Rückweg, Öl auf Leinwand
Le Retour, huile sur toile
De terugkeer (Le retour), olieverf op doek
1940
50 x 65 cm / 19.6 x 25.5 in.
Musées Royaux des Beaux-Arts, Brussel

◀ **René Magritte**
(Lessen 1898 - Brussel 1967)
L'avenir des statues, oil on canvas
Die Zukunft der Statuen, Öl auf Leinwand
L'Avenir des statues, huile sur toile
De toekomst van de beelden, olieverf op doek
1932
h. 32 cm / 12.5 in.
Wilhelm Lehmbruck Museum, Duisburg

▶ **René Magritte**
(Lessen 1898 - Brussel 1967)
Edward James 'On the Threshold of Liberty,
gelatin silver print
Edward James vor das 'On the Threshold of Liberty,
Silbergelatinedruck
Edward James devant On the Threshold of Liberty,
épreuve gélatino-argentique
Edward James voor 'On the Threshold of Liberty',
gelatinezilverafdruk
1937
10,8 x 16,7 cm / 4.2 x 6.5 in.
Metropolitan Museum of Art, New York

Alberto Savinio
(Athína 1891 - Roma 1952)
In the forest, oil on canvas
Im Wald, Öl auf Leinwand
Dans la forêt, huile sur toile
In het woud, olieverf op doek
1928
81 x 65 cm / 31.8 x 25.5 in.
Private Collection / Privatsammlung / Collection privée / Privécollectie

▶ **Alberto Savinio**
(Athína 1891 - Roma 1952)
The graces of the island, oil on canvas
Die Grazien der Insel, Öl auf Leinwand
L'île des charmes charmes de l'île, huile sur toile
De gratiën van het eiland, olieverf op doek
1928
Private Collection / Privatsammlung / Collection privée / Privécollectie

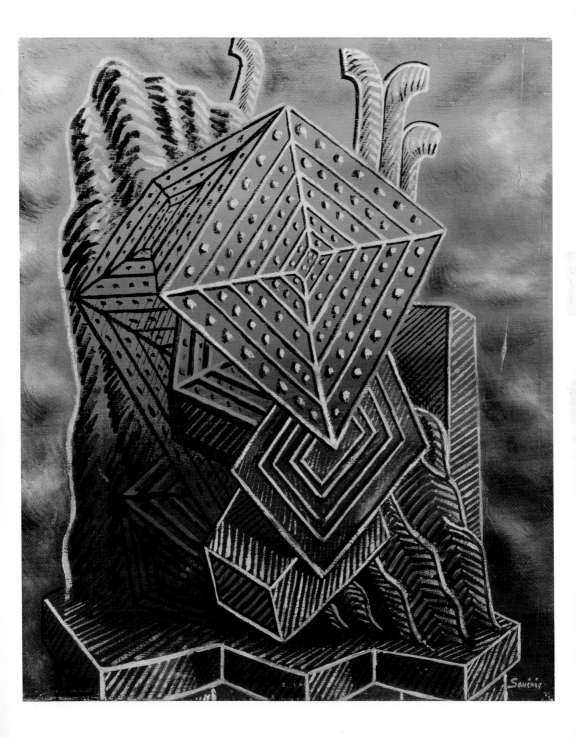

Alberto Savinio
(Athina 1891 - Roma 1952)
Orpheus and Eurydice, oil on canvas
Orpheus und Eurydike, Öl auf Leinwand
Orphée et Eurydice, huile sur toile
Orpheus en Euridice, olieverf op doek
c. 1940
82 x 66 cm / 32.2 x 25.9 in.
Galleria d'Arte Moderna di Palazzo Pitti, Firenze

Alberto Savinio
(Athína 1891 - Roma 1952)
Objects in the forest, oil on canvas
Gegenstände im Wald, Öl auf Leinwand
Objets dans la forêt, huile sur toile
Objecten in het bos, olieverf op doek
1926-1928
Private Collection / Privatsammlung / Collection privée / Privécollectie

Frida Kahlo
(Coyoacán, Ciudad de México 1907 - 1954)
A few small jabs, oil on canvas
Einige kleine Stiche, Öl auf Leinwand
Quelques petites piqûres, huile sur toile
Een paar prikjes, olieverf op doek
1935
Fundación Dolores Olmedo, Ciudad de México

◀ **Frida Kahlo**
(Coyoacán, Ciudad de México 1907 - 1954)
What the water gave me, oil on canvas
Das was mir das Wasser gab, Öl auf Leinwand
Ce que l'eau m'a donné, huile sur toile
Wat het water me gaf, olieverf op doek
1935
Collection Isadore Ducasse, Fine Arts Museum, New York

The betrayal of images

In the best tradition of the Flemish masters of the Renaissance and close on the example of De Chirico and the Italian Metaphysical painters the Surrealists depicted absurd environments, at once disturbing and mysterious. Pictorial space appeared dilated while figures and settings became isolated in desolate clarity. Such gelid worlds responded to the sense of disorientation and dismay felt by many observers, recognising the power of enigma.

Der Verrat der Bilder

Nach bester Tradition der niederländischen Meister der Renaissance und nach dem Beispiel von De Chirico und der italienischen Metaphysik, entstehen absurde, ja beunruhigende und geheimnisvolle Atmosphären. Der dargestellte Raum weitet sich aus, die Figuren und Szenen erscheinen ausführlich und absolut klar. Dennoch, einer so eiskalten Definition entspricht die Verwirrung und Unruhe des Beobachters. Macht des Mysteriums.

La trahison des images

Dans la meilleure tradition des maîtres flamands de la Renaissance et dans le sillage de l'Italien De Chirico et de sa peinture « métaphysique » naissent ainsi des atmosphères absurdes et mystérieuses, voire inquiétantes. L'espace pictural se dilate tandis que personnages et mises en scène paraissent déterminés avec une clarté impitoyable. Et pourtant, cette définition si glaciale suscite en écho le dépaysement et le désarroi du spectateur. Pouvoir de l'énigme.

Het verraad van de beelden

Volgens de traditie van de Vlaamse meesters van de Renaissance en naar het voorbeeld van De Chirico en de Italiaanse Metafysica, ontstaan absurde, dan niet verontrustende en mysterieuze atmosferen. De beeldruimte breidt zich uit, terwijl figuren en decors omringd lijken te zijn met onbetwistbare helderheid. Niettemin komt de koele benadering overeen met de disoriëntatie en de verwarring van de toeschouwer. De kracht van het enigma.

3

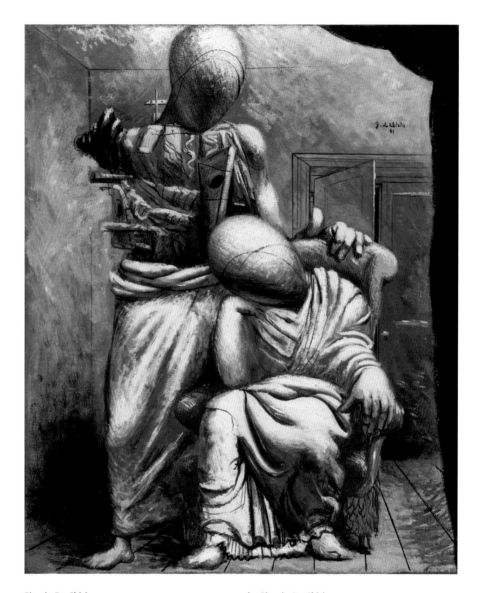

Giorgio De Chirico
(Vólos 1888 - Roma 1978)
The poet and his muse, oil and tempera on canvas
Der Dichter und seine Muse, Öl und Tempera auf Leinwand
Le Poète consolé par sa muse, huile et détrempe sur toile
De dichter en zijn muze, tempera en olieverf op doek
1921
91,1 x 73,7 cm / 35.8 x 29 in.
Philadelphia Museum of Art, Philadelphia

▶ **Giorgio De Chirico**
(Vólos 1888 - Roma 1978)
The great metaphysical, oil on canvas
Der große Metaphysiker, Öl auf Leinwand
Le grand Métaphysicien, huile sur toile
De grote metafysicus, olieverf op doek
1924-1926
110 x 80 cm / 43.3 x 31.4 in.
Nationalgalerie, Staatliche Museen zu Berlin, Berlin

Giorgio De Chirico
(Vólos 1888 - Roma 1978)
Metaphysical interior, oil on canvas
Metaphysisches Innere, Öl auf Leinwand
Intérieur métaphysique, huile sur toile
Metafysisch interieur, olieverf op doek
1925
71 x 55 cm / 27.9 x 21.6 in.
Yale University Art Gallery, New Haven

Paul Delvaux
(Antheit 1897 - Furnes 1994)
The phases of the moon, oil on canvas
Phasen des Mondes, Öl auf Leinwand
Les Phases de la lune, huile sur toile
De fasen van de maan, olieverf op doek
1939
139,7 x 160 cm / 54.9 x 62.9 in.
Museum of Modern Art, New York

Paul Delvaux
(Antheit 1897 - Furnes 1994)
The stairway, oil on canvas
Die Treppe, Öl auf Leinwand
L'Escalier, huile sur toile
De trap, olieverf op doek
1946
122 x 152,5 cm / 48 x 60 in.
Museum voor Schone Kunsten, Gent

Paul Delvaux
(Antheit 1897 - Furnes 1994)
The great sirens, oil on masonite
Die drei großen Sirenen, Öl auf Hartfaserplatte
Les Grandes Sirènes, huile sur masonite
De grote sirenen, olieverf op masoniet
1947
305 x 203 cm / 120 x 90.5 in.
Metropolitan Museum of Art, New York

Paul Delvaux
(Antheit 1897 - Furnes 1994)
The Acropolis, oil on canvas
Die Akropolis, Öl auf Leinwand
L'Acropole, huile sur toile
Acropolis, olieverf op doek
1966
150 x 230 cm / 59 x 90.5 in.
Centre Georges Pompidou, Musée National d'Art Moderne, Paris

▶ **Salvador Dalí**
(Figueres 1904 - 1989)
Portrait of Mrs Isabel Styler-Tas (Melancholy), oil on canvas
Porträt der Frau Isabel Styler-Tas (Melencolia), Öl auf Leinwand
Portrait de Madame Isabel Styler-Tas (Melancolia), huile sur toile
Portret van mevrouw Isabel Styler-Tas (Melancholie), olieverf op doek
1945
65,5 x 86 cm / 25.7 x 33.8 in.
Nationalgalerie, Staatliche Museen zu Berlin, Berlin

Max Ernst
(Brühl 1891 - Paris 1976)
Gartenblumen, oil and collage on canvas
Gartenblumen, Öl und Collage auf Leinwand
Gartenblumen, huile et collage sur toile
Gartenblumen, olieverf en collage op doek
1926
65 x 81 cm / 25.5 x 31.8 in.
Hamburger Kunsthalle, Hamburg

▶ **Max Ernst**
(Brühl 1891 - Paris 1976)
Figure and bird
Figur und Vogel
Figure et oiseau
Figuur en vogel
Collezione Thyssen, Lugano

Max Ernst
(Brühl 1891 - Paris 1976)
Chimera, oil on canvas
Chimäre, Öl auf Leinwand
Chimère, huile sur toile
Chimera, olieverf op doek
1928
114 x 146 cm / 44.8 x 57.4 in.
Centre Georges Pompidou, Musée National d'Art Moderne, Paris

▶ **Max Ernst**
(Brühl 1891 - Paris 1976)
Cypresses, oil on canvas
Zypressen, Öl auf Leinwand
Cyprès, huile sur toile
Cipressen, olieverf op doek
1939
44 x 30 cm / 17.3 x 11.8 in.
Hamburger Kunsthalle, Hamburg

Balthus
(Paris 1908 - Rossinière 2001)
Portrait of André Derain, oil on wood
Porträt des André Derain, Öl auf Holz
Portrait d'André Derain, huile sur bois
Portret van André Derain, olieverf op hout
1936
112,7 x 72,4 cm / 44.3 x 28.5 in.
Museum of Modern Art, New York

Balthus
(Paris 1908 - Rossinière 2001)
Joan Miró with his daughter Dolores, oil on canvas
Joan Miró mit Tochter Dolores, Öl auf Leinwand
Joan Miró et sa fille Dolorès, huile sur toile
Joan Miró met zijn dochter Dolores, olieverf op doek
1937-1938
130,2 x 88,9 cm / 51.2 x 34.9 in.
Museum of Modern Art, New York

René Magritte
(Lessen 1898 - Brussel 1967)
The betrayal of images, oil on canvas
Der Verrat der Bilder, Öl auf Leinwand
La Trahison des images, huile sur toile
Het verraad van de beelden, olieverf op doek
1929
60 x 81 cm / 23.6 x 31.8 in.
County Museum of Art, Los Angeles

◀ **René Magritte**
(Lessen 1898 - Brussel 1967)
Untitled, collage: paper, wash, pencil on paper
Ohne Titel, Collage: Papier, Aquarell, Bleistift auf Papier
Sans titre, collage : papier, aquarelle et mine de plomb sur papier
Zonder titel, collage: papier, aquarel, potlood op papier
1926
56,5 x 40,5 cm / 22.2 x 15.9 in.
Private Collection / Privatsammlung / Collection privée / Privécollectie

René Magritte
(Lessen 1898 - Brussel 1967)
The alphabet of revelations, oil on canvas
Das Alphabet der Offenbarungen, Öl auf Leinwand
L'Alphabet des révélations, huile sur toile
Het alfabet van de openbaringen (L'alphabet des révélations), olieverf op doek
1929
54 x 73 cm / 23.6 x 31.8 in.
The Menil Collection, Houston

▶ **René Magritte**
(Lessen 1898 - Brussel 1967)
The human condition, oil on canvas
Menschliche Bedingungen, Öl auf Leinwand
La Condition humaine, huile sur toile
Het menselijk tekort (La condition humaine), olieverf op doek
1932
100 x 81 cm / 39.3 x 31.8 in.
National Gallery of Art, Washington

René Magritte
(Lessen 1898 - Brussel 1967)
Georgette
Oil and pencil on canvas
Öl und Bleistift auf Leinwand
Huile et mine de plomb sur toile
Olieverf en potlood op doek
1935
65 x 75 cm / 25.5 x 29.5 in.
Private Collection / Privatsammlung / Collection privée / Privécollectie

René Magritte
(Lessen 1898 - Brussel 1967)
The revenge, oil on canvas
Die Rache, Öl auf Leinwand
La Vengeance, huile sur toile
De wraak, olieverf op doek
1936
54 x 65 cm / 21.2 x 25.5 in.
Private Collection / Privatsammlung / Collection privée / Privécollectie

René Magritte
(Lessen 1898 - Brussel 1967)
Painted object, oil on wood
Bemaltes Objekt, Öl auf Holz
Objet peint, huile sur bois
Beschilderd object, olieverf op hout
1936
25 x 25 x 25 cm; ø 15,3 cm / 9.8 x 9.8 x 9.8 in.; ø 6 in.
Private Collection / Privatsammlung / Collection privée / Privécollectie

▶ **René Magritte**
(Lessen 1898 - Brussel 1967)
Le modele rouge, oil on canvas
Das rote Modell, Öl auf Leinwand
Le Modèle rouge, huile sur toile
Le modele rouge, olieverf op doek
1937
180 x 134 cm / 70.8 x 52.7 in.
Museum Boymans van Beuningen, Rotterdam

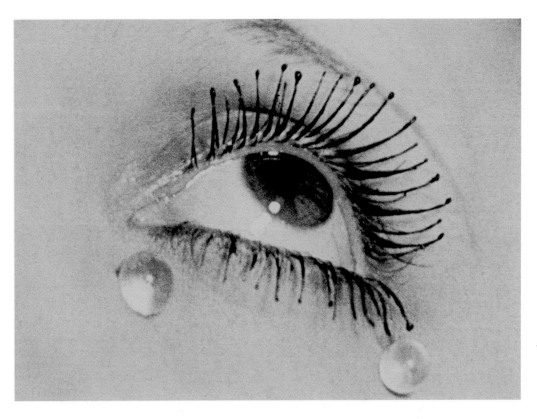

Man Ray
(Philadelphia 1890 - Paris 1976)
Tears (Tears of glass), black and white photograph
Tränen (Glastränen), Schwarzweiß-Bild
Larmes (Larmes de verre), photographie en noir et blanc
Tranen (Tranen van glas), zwart-wit foto
1932
18 x 24 cm / 7 x 9.4 in.
Private Collection / Privatsammlung / Collection privée / Privécollectie

◀ **Man Ray**
(Philadelphia 1890 - Paris 1976)
Promenade, oil on canvas
Promenade, Öl auf Leinwand
Promenade, huile sur toile
Promenade, olieverf op doek
1941
152,4 x 102,2 cm / 59.9 x 40.2 in.
Yale University Art Gallery, New Haven

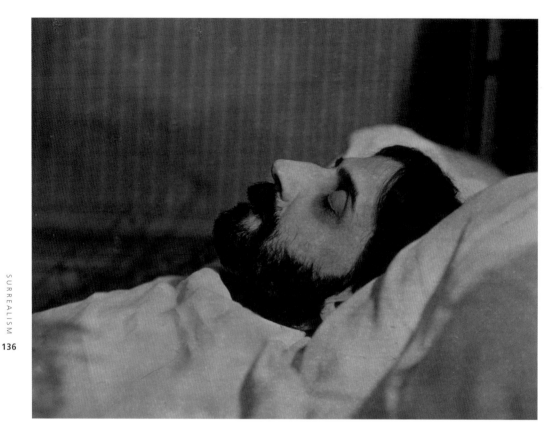

Man Ray
(Philadelphia 1890 - Paris 1976)
Marcel Proust on his deathbed, taken on the eve of the funeral, Monday 20 November 1922, black and white photograph
Marcel Proust auf dem Totenbett, Aufgenommen am Montag, dem 20. November 1922, Schwarzweiß-Bild
Marcel Proust sur son lit de mort. Photo prise la veille des funérailles, lundi 20 novembre 1922, photographie en noir et blanc
Marcel Proust op zijn doodsbed, op de avond voor de begrafenis, maandag 20 november 1922, zwart-wit foto
15,5 x 20,2 cm / 6.1 x 7.9 in.
Musée d'Orsay, Paris

▶ **Man Ray**
(Philadelphia 1890 - Paris 1976)
Le pont transbordeur, black and white photograph
Die Transbordeur Brücke, Schwarzweiß-Bild
Le Pont transbordeur, photographie en noir et blanc
De zweefbrug, zwart-wit foto
1936
14 x 8,9 cm / 5.5 x 3.5 in.
Musée Cantini, Marseille

Frida Kahlo
(Coyoacán, Ciudad de México 1907 - 1954)
The two Fridas, oil on canvas
Die zwei Fridas, Öl auf Leinwand
Les deux Frida, huile sur toile
De twee Frida's, olieverf op doek
1939
67 x 67 cm / 26.3 x 26.3 in.
Museo Nacional de Arte Moderno,
Ciudad de México

▶ **Frida Kahlo**
(Coyoacán, Ciudad de México 1907 - 1954)
My grandparents, my parents and me (genealogical tree), oil and tempera on a metal panel
Meine Großeltern, meine Eltern und Ich (Stammbaum), Öl und Tempera auf Metallplatte
Mes grands-parents, mes parents et moi (arbre généalogique), huile et détrempe sur panneau métallique
Mijn grootouders, mijn ouders en ik (stamboom), olieverf en tempera op metaalpaneel
1936
30,7 x 34,5 cm / 12 x 13.5 in.
Museum of Modern Art, New York

▶ **Frida Kahlo**
(Coyoacán, Ciudad de México 1907 - 1954)
My nanny and me, oil on metal
Meine Amme und Ich (Mi Nana y yo), Öl auf Metall
Ma nourrice et moi, huile sur metal
Mijn Tata en ik (Mi Nana y yo), olieverf op metaal
1937
30,5 x 34,7 cm / 12 x 13.6 in.
Fundación Dolores Olmedo, Ciudad de México

Henry Moore
(Castleford 1898 - Much Hadham 1986)
Bird Basket, lignum vitae and string
Vogelkorb (Bird Basket), Lignum vitae und Seile
Bird Basket, lignum vitae et corde
Vogelmand (Bird Basket), lignum vitae en koord
1939
42 cm / 16.53 in.
Henry Moore Foundation, Much Hadham

▶ **Henry Moore**
(Castleford 1898 - Much Hadham 1986)
Figure, corsehill stone
Figur, Corsehill-Stein
Figure, pierre de corsehill
Figuur, steen uit corsehill
1933-1934
h. 76 cm / 29.9 in.
Private Collection / Privatsammlung / Collection privée / Privécollectie

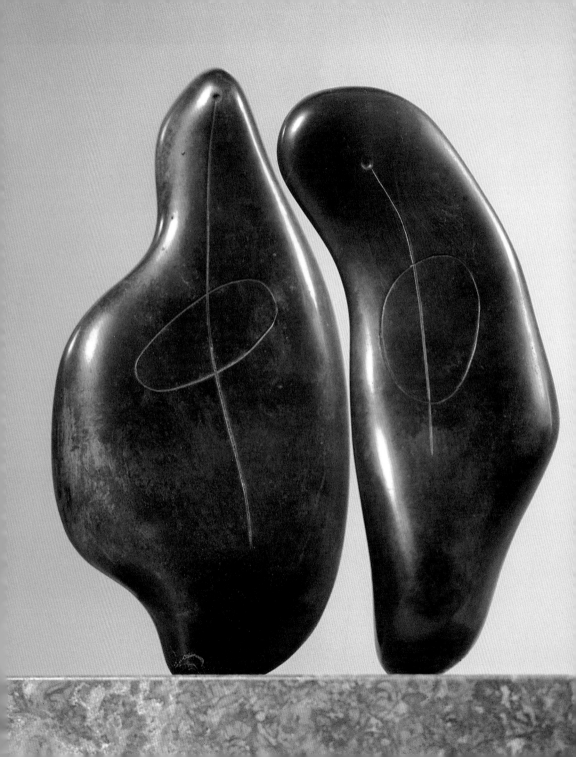

Henry Moore
(Castleford 1898 - Much Hadham 1986)
Reclining figure, alabaster
Liegende Figur, Alabaster
Figure étendue, albâtre
Liggende figuur, albast
1929
47 cm / 18.5 in.
Private Collection / Privatsammlung / Collection privée /
Privécollectie

◀ **Henry Moore**
(Castleford 1898 - Much Hadham 1986)
Two pieces, bronze
Bi-Form, Bronze
Bi-forme, bronze
Bi-forma, brons
1933-1934
18,5 cm / 7.2 in.
Henry Moore Foundation, Much Hadham

▌ *"I am very much aware that associational, psychological factors, play a large part in sculpture. The meaning and significance of form itself probably depends on the countless associations of man's history"*
▌ *"Ich bin mir der Rolle der psychologischen Faktoren und der gedanklichen Assoziationen in der Bildhauerei vollends bewusst. Der Sinn der Form ist von den unendlichen Assoziationen nicht trennbar, die sich im Laufe der menschlichen Geschichte um sie herum angehäuft haben."*
▌ *« Je suis parfaitement conscient du rôle que jouent les facteurs psychologiques et les associations d'idées dans la sculpture. On ne peut séparer le sens de la forme, des associations infinies qui, au cours de l'histoire de l'humanité, se sont accumulées autour d'elle. »*
▌ *"Ik ben mij volkomen bewust van de rol die de psychologische factoren en de ideeënassociatie in de beeldhouwkunst spelen. Het nut van de vorm is niet te scheiden van de oneindige associaties, die zich in de loop van de geschiedenis van de mens, om haar heen heeft verzameld."*
Henry Moore

Disquiet. Eroticism and analysis

Devoid of logic and reason, playful and absurd: the world depicted by the Surrealists was one turned upside down. The rules governing bourgeois life were rejected to make way for eroticism and the provocation of desire. The suppressed comes to the surface; the object of desire is revealed, shameless, shocking and amoral, without any strictures.

Das Unheimliche. Erotismus und Tiefenanalyse

Unlogisch, irrational, spielerisch, absurd: das von den Surrealisten zelebrierte Universum scheint eine Kopfüberwelt zu sein; hier sind die Regeln des bürgerlichen Lebens geächtet und das bedingungslose erotische Verlangen triumphiert in seiner deklamierten Provokation. Das Verdrängte kommt an die Oberfläche, das Objekt der Begierde offenbart sich schamlos, schockierend, unmoralisch, unkontrolliert.

4

Le troublant. Érotisme et psychologie des profondeurs

Alogique, absurde, irrationnel et ludique: l'univers célébré à l'envi par les surréalistes semble un monde à l'envers d'où sont bannies les normes de la vie bourgeoise et où le désir érotique triomphe sans partage, dans sa provocation délibérée et revendiquée. Le refoulé surgit, envahissant ; « cet obscur objet du désir » (Buñuel) se révèle, impudique et choquant, immoral et affranchi de tout contrôle.

De ontwrichting. Erotiek en diepgaande analyse

Onlogisch, irrationeel, speels en absurd: het door surrealisten gevierde universum lijkt op een omgekeerde wereld, waar de normen van het burgerlijke leven zijn verworpen en waar het erotische verlangen in haar uitgesproken provocatie onvoorwaardelijk zegeviert. Het onderdrukte doemt op en het onderwerp van verlangen onthult zich obsceen, choquerend, immoreel en ongecontroleerd.

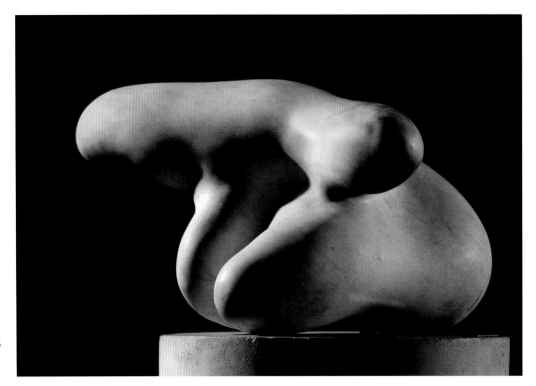

Jean (Hans) Arp
(Strasbourg 1887 - Basel 1966)
Human concretion, marble
Menschliche Konkretion, Marmor
Concrétion humaine (torse-fruit), marbre
Menselijke concretie, marmer
1934
32 x 56 x 43 cm / 12.5 x 22 x 16.9 in.
Centre Georges Pompidou, Musée National d'Art Moderne, Paris

Jean (Hans) Arp
(Strasbourg 1887 - Basel 1966)
Human concretion, plaster
Menschliche Konkretion, Gips
Concrétion humaine, plâtre
Menselijke concretie, gips
1935
49,5 x 47,6 x 64,7 cm / 19.4 x 18.7 x 25.4 in.
Museum of Modern Art, New York

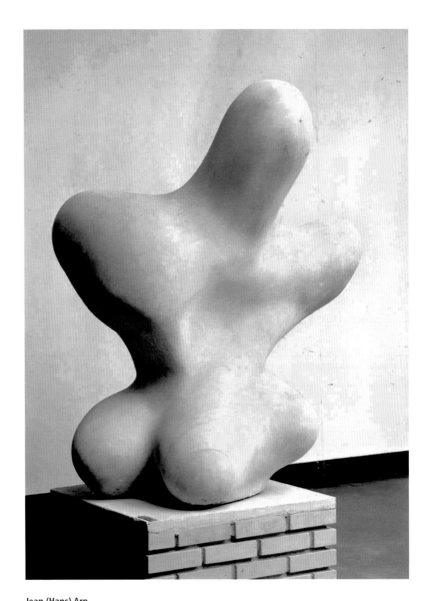

Jean (Hans) Arp
(Strasbourg 1887 - Basel 1966)
Big seed, marble
Großer Kern, Marmor
Pépin géant, marbre
De grote Pepin, marmer
1937
162 x 127 x 77 cm / 63.7 x 49.9 x 30.3 in.
Centre Georges Pompidou, Musée National d'Art Moderne, Paris

Hans Bellmer
(Kattowitz 1902 - Paris 1975)
The doll. Variations, black and white photograph
Die Puppe. Variationen, Schwarzweiß- Bild
La poupée. Variations, photographie en noir et blanc
De pop. Variaties, zwart-wit foto
1933
19,5 x 30 cm / 7.6 x 11.8 in.
Musée Cantini, Marseille

Hans Bellmer
(Kattowitz 1902 - Paris 1975)
The doll. Variations, photograph
Die Puppe. Variationen, Bild
La poupée. Variations, photographie
De pop. Variaties, zwart-wit foto
1934
19,5 x 30 cm / 7.6 x 11.8 in.
Private Collection / Privatsammlung /
Collection privée / Privécollectie

Salvador Dalí
(Figueres 1904 - 1989)
Spectral cow, painting and oil on canvas
Spektrale Kuh, Ölfarben auf Leinwand
La Vache spectrale, peinture à l'huile sur contreplaquè
Spectrale koeien, olieverf op doek
1928
50 x 64.5 cm / 19.6 x 25.3 in.
Centre Georges Pompidou, Musée National d'Art Moderne, Paris

Salvador Dalí
(Figueres 1904 - 1989)
Illuminated pleasures, oil and collage on board
Erleuchtete Lüste, Öl und Collage auf Pappe
Les Plaisirs illuminés, huile et collage sur carton
Verlichte genoegens, olieverf en collage op bordpapier
1929
23,8 x 34,7 cm / 9.3 x 13.6 in.
Museum of Modern Art, New York

Salvador Dalí
(Figueres 1904 - 1989)
The old age of William Tell, oil on canvas
Das Greisenalter des Wilhelm Tell, Öl auf Leinwand
La Vieillesse de Guillaume Tell, huile sur toile
De ouderdom van Wilhelm Tell, olieverf op doek
1931
98 x 140 cm / 38.5 x 55.1 in.
Private Collection / Privatsammlung / Collection privée / Privécollectie

▶ **Salvador Dalí**
(Figueres 1904 - 1989)
Bust of a retrospective woman, painted porcelain and assemblage
Retrospektive Frauenbüste, bemaltes Porzelan und Assemblage
Buste de femme rétrospectif, porcelaine peinte et assemblage d'objets variés
Buste van een vrouw in retrospectief, beschilderd porselein en assemblage van verschillende voorwerpen
1933
73,9 x 69,2 x 32 cm / 29 x 27.2 x 12.5 in.
Museum of Modern Art, New York

Max Ernst
(Brühl 1891 - Paris 1976)
Woman, old man and a flower, oil on canvas
Frau, alter Mann und Blume, Öl auf Leinwand
Femme, vieillard et fleur, huile sur toile
Vrouw, oude man en bloem, olieverf op doek
1923-1924
96,5 x 130,2 cm / 37.9 x 51.2 in.
Museum of Modern Art, New York

◀ **Salvador Dalí**
(Figueres 1904 - 1989)
Portrait of Gala (The Angelus of Gala), oil on panel
Porträt von Gala (Der Angelus von Gala), Öl auf Tafel
Portrait de Gala (L'Angélus de Gala), huile sur panneau
Portret van Gala (L'Angelus de Gala), olieverf op paneel
1935
32,4 x 26,7 cm / 12.7 x 10.5 in.
Museum of Modern Art, New York

Joseph Cornell
(Nyack, New York 1903 - New York 1972)
Untitled (Baby Marie), assemblage of various
objects in a wooden box
Ohne Titel (Baby Marie), Assemblage
von verschiedenen Gegenstände in einer
Holzschachtel
Sans titre (Bébé Marie), assemblage d'objets
divers, dans une boîte de bois
Zonder titel (Bebe' Marie), assemblage van
verschillende voorwerpen in een kist
c. 1941
59,7 x 31,5 x 13,3 cm / 23.5 x 12.4 x 5.2 in.
Museum of Modern Art, New York

▶ **Max Ernst**
(Brühl 1891 - Paris 1976)
Alice in 1941, oil on paper mounted on
canvas
Alice, 1941, Öl auf Papier aufgetragen auf
Leinwand
Alice en 1941, huile sur papier, marouflée
sur toile
Alice in 1941, olieverf op papier op doek
1941
40 x 32,3 cm / 15.7 x 12.7 in.
Museum of Modern Art, New York

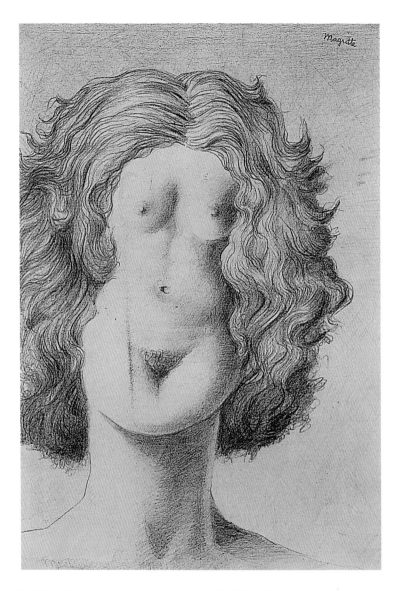

René Magritte
(Lessen 1898 - Brussel 1967)
Rape, pencil on paper
Die Vergewaltigung, Bleistift auf Papier
Le Viol, mine de plomb sur papier
De verkrachting (Le viol), potlood op papier
1934
36,5 x 25 cm / 14.3 x 9.8 in.
The Menil Collection, Houston

▶ **René Magritte**
(Lessen 1898 - Brussel 1967)
Rape, oil on canvas
Die Vergewaltigung, Öl auf Leinwand
Le Viol, huile sur toile
De verkrachting (Le viol), olieverf op doek
1934
73 x 54 cm / 28.7 x 21.2 in.
The Menil Collection, Houston

René Magritte
(Lessen 1898 - Brussel 1967)
The sleepwalker, oil on canvas
Der Schlafwandler, Öl auf Leinwand
Le Somnambule, huile sur toile
De slaapwandelaar, olieverf op doek
1946
54 x 65 cm / 21.2 x 25.5 in.
Private Collection / Privatsammlung / Collection privée / Privécollectie

◀ **René Magritte**
(Lessen 1898 - Brussel 1967)
Black magic, oil on canvas
Schwarze Magie, Öl auf Leinwand
Magie noire, huile sur toile
Zwarte magie, olieverf op doek
1945
80 x 60 cm / 31.4 x 23.6 in.
Musées Royaux des Beaux-Arts de Belgique, Brussel

Man Ray
(Philadelphia 1890 - Paris 1976)
Princess Murat and the moon rise on the Island of Nias
Die Prinzessin Murat und der Mond, erheben sich über die Insel Nias
La Princesse Murat, et La lune se lève sur l'île de Nias
Op het eiland Nias richten prinses Murat en de maan zich op

▶ **Man Ray**
(Philadelphia 1890 - Paris 1976)
Le Violon d'Ingres, gelatin silver print altered in printing
Die Violine von Ingres, Silbergelatinedruck, während des Druckvorgangs verändert
Le Violon d'Ingres, épreuve gélatino-argentique montée sur papier, retravaillée au tirage
Le Violon d'Ingres, gelatinezilverdruk bewerkt tijdens het drukprocedé
1924
30 x 24 cm / 11.8 x 9.4 in.
Centre Georges Pompidou, Musée National d'Art Moderne, Paris

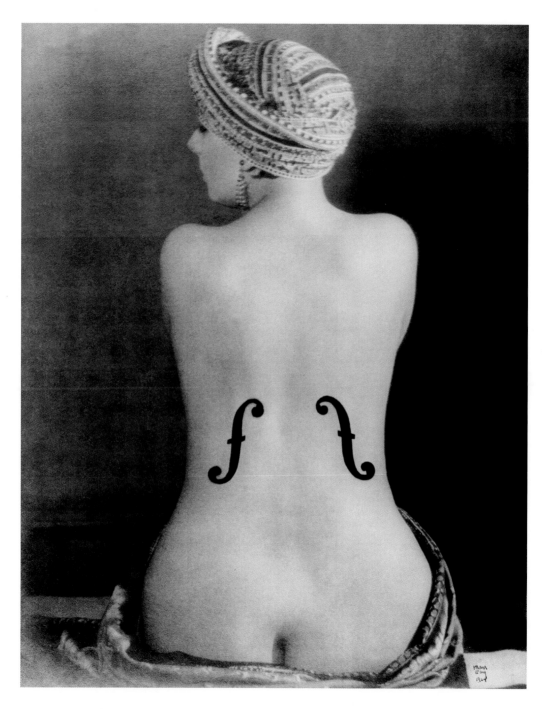

Man Ray
(Philadelphia 1890 - Paris 1976)
Rose
Gelatin silver print
Silbergelatinedruck
Épreuve gélatino-argentique
Gelatinezilverdruk
1929
29,7 x 23,2 cm / 11.6 x 9.1 in.
Private Collection / Privatsammlung /
Collection privée / Privécollectie

▶ **Man Ray**
(Philadelphia 1890 - Paris 1976)
Lee Miller
1930

Pablo Picasso
(Málaga 1881 - Mougins 1973)
Dora Maar in an armchair, oil on canvas
Dora Maar im Sessel, Öl auf Leinwand
Portrait de Dora Maar dans un fauteuil, huile sur toile
Dora Maar in een leunstoel, olieverf op doek
1939
73,3 x 60,3 cm / 28.8 x 23.7 in.
Metropolitan Museum of Art, New York

▶ **Pablo Picasso**
(Málaga 1881 - Mougins 1973)
Woman dressing her hair, oil on canvas
Frau, ihre Haare richtend, Öl auf Leinwand
Femme se coiffant, huile sur toile
Vrouw die haar haren kamt, olieverf op doek
1940
130,1 x 97,1 cm / 51.2 x 38.2 in.
Museum of Modern Art, New York

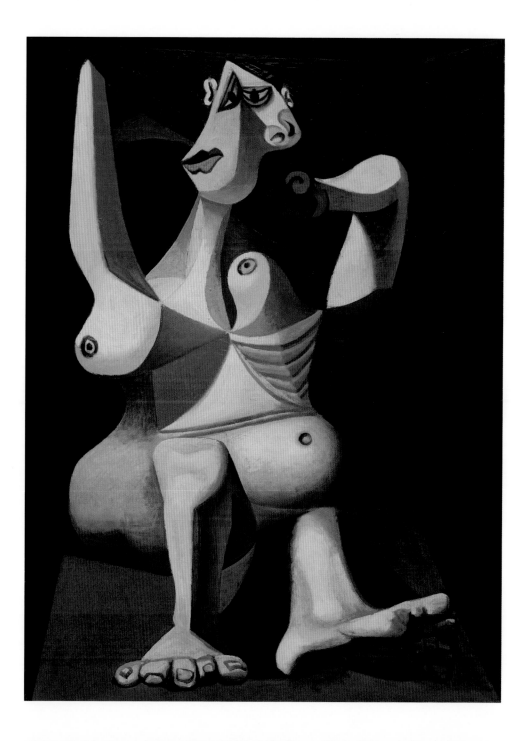

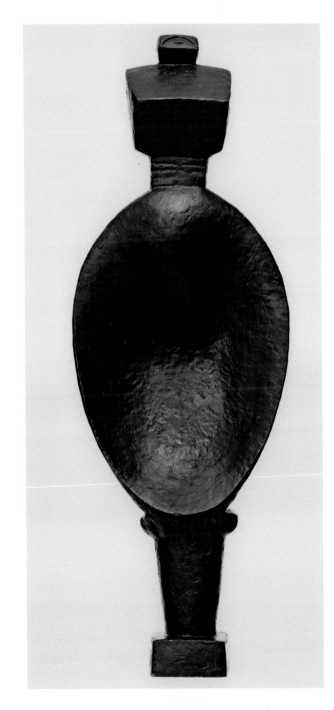

Alberto Giacometti
(Borgonovo di Stampa 1901 - Chur 1966)
Woman-spoon, bronze
Löffelfrau, Bronze
Femme-cuillère, bronze
Lepel-vrouw, brons
1926-1927
144,8 x 51,4 x 21 cm / 57 x 20.2 x 8.2 in.
Museum of Modern Art, New York

◀ **Alberto Savinio**
(Athína 1891 - Roma 1952)
Annunciation, oil on canvas
Die Verkündigung, Öl auf Leinwand
L'Annonciation, huile sur toile
Annunciatie, olieverf op doek
1932
81 x 65 cm / 31.8 x 25.2 in.
Private Collection / Privatsammlung /
Collection privée / Privécollectie

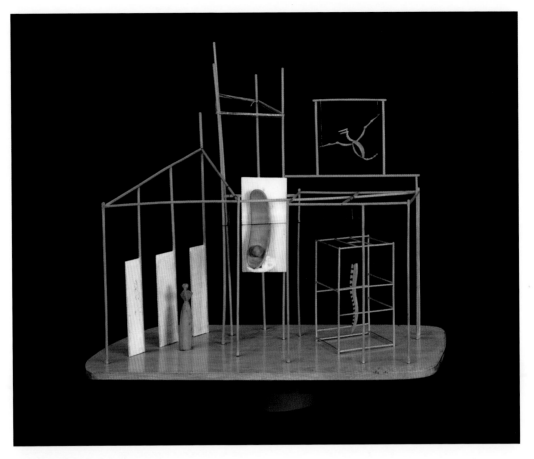

Alberto Giacometti
(Borgonovo di Stampa 1901 - Chur 1966)
The building at four in the morning, construction in wood, glass, mixed materials
Palast um vier Uhr morgens, Konstruktion aus Holz, Glas, verschiedenen Materialien
Le Palais à quatre heures du matin, construction en bois, verre et matériaux divers
Het paleis om vier uur 's ochtends, constructie van hout, glas en diverse materialen
1932-1933
63,5 x 71,8 x 40 cm / 9 x 28.2 x 15.7 in.
Museum of Modern Art, New York

◄ **Alberto Giacometti**
(Borgonovo di Stampa 1901 - Chur 1966)
The couple, bronze
Das Paar, Bronze
Le Couple, bronze
Het paar, brons
1926
59,7 x 36,88 x 7,8 cm / 23.5 x 14.4 x 3 in.
Museum of Modern Art, New York

Alberto Giacometti
(Borgonovo di Stampa 1901 - Chur 1966)
Woman with her throat cut, bronze
Frau mit durchgeschnittener Kehle, Bronze
Femme à la gorge tranchée, bronze
Vrouw met doorgesneden hals, brons
1932
20,3 x 87,6 x 63,5 cm / 7.9 x 34.4 x 24.9 in.
Museum of Modern Art, New York

▶ **Alberto Giacometti**
(Borgonovo di Stampa 1901 - Chur 1966)
Hands holding the void, plaster
Hände, die Leere haltend, Gips
Mains tenant le vide, plâtre
Handen die de leegte vasthouden, gesso (gips)
1934
156,2 x 34,3 x 29.2 cm / 61.4 x 13.5 x 11.4 in.
Yale University Art Gallery, New Haven

Paul Horst
(Weißenfels 1906 - Palm Beach 1999)
Costume for 'The dream of Venus' by Salvador Dalí, gelatin silver print
Kostüm für 'Der Traum der Venus' von Salvador Dalí, Silbergelatinedruck
Costume pour 'Le Rêve de Vénus' de Salvador Dalí, épreuve gélatino-argentique
Kostuum voor 'Il Sogno di Venere' van Salvador Dalí, gelatinezilverdruk
1939
25 x 19,1 cm / 9.8 x 7.5 in.
Museum of Modern Art, New York

▶ **Paul Horst**
(Weißenfels 1906 - Palm Beach 1999)
Costume for , 'The dream of Venus' by Salvador Dalí, gelatin silver print
Kostüm für 'Der Traum der Venus' von Salvador Dalí, Silbergelatinedruck
Costume pour 'Le Rêve de Vénus' de Salvador Dalí, épreuve gélatino-argentique
Kostuum voor 'Il Sogno di Venere' van Salvador Dalí, gelatinezilverdruk
1939
19 x 25,4 cm / 7.4 x 9.9 in.
Museum of Modern Art, New York

Meret Oppenheim
(Berlin 1913 - Basel 1985)
Object (Le dejeuner en fourrure), fur cup, plate, and spoon
Objekt (Frühstück im Pelz), Tasse, Teller und Löffel mit Pelz umkleidet
Le Déjeuner en fourrure, tasse, assiette et cuillère revêtues de fourrure
Object (Le dejeuner en fourrure), kopje, bord en lepeltje, bekleed met bont
1936
h. 7,3 cm / 2.87 in.
Museum of Modern Art, New York

◀ **Francis Picabia**
(Paris 1879 - 1953)
Les seins, oil on board
Die Brüste, Öl auf Karton
Les Seins, huile sur carton
De boezem, olieverf op karton
1924
99 x 75,5 cm / 38.9 x 29.7 in.
Private Collection / Privatsammlung / Collection privée / Privécollectie

Evolutions

As the old Europe was subjected to the rule of dictators and the horrors of war Surrealism crossed the Atlantic where Man Ray, Duchamp and others were sought out by American collectors and by adventurous young artists. In the post-war years the artistic scene was no longer Paris but New York where new movements would take up the surrealists' promotion of psychic automatism, the release of the subconscious and unfettered thought.

Evolutionen

Während das alte Europa unter den Zerstörungen der Diktaturen und dann der Kriege leidet, wandert der Surrealismus in die Vereinigten Staaten aus, wo Man Ray, Duchamp und die anderen von scharfsinnigen Sammlern und jungen unternehmungslustigen Künstlern sehnsüchtig erwartet werden. In der Nachkriegszeit wechselt also die Künstlerszene von Paris nach New York, wo eine neue Geschichte ihren Anfang nimmt. Die neue Konfrontation gründet sich auf den psychischen Automatismus, auf das bedingungslose Hochkommen des Unterbewussten, auf die Freiheit der surrealistischen Meister.

5

Évolutions

Tandis que la « vieille » Europe s'étiole sous les coups des dictatures puis de la guerre, le surréalisme émigre aux États-Unis où Duchamp, Man Ray et les autres sont attendus par des collectionneurs avertis et par de jeunes artistes entreprenants. L'après-guerre verra donc la scène artistique se déplacer de Paris à New York où une nouvelle histoire va commencer. Les recherches nouvelles se fonderont largement sur les automatismes psychiques, sur la révélation inconditionnée du refoulé - en un mot : sur la liberté souveraine des maîtres du surréalisme.

Ontwikkelingen

Terwijl het oude Europa eerst wegkwijnt onder de klappen van de dictatuur en vervolgens van de oorlog, migreert het Surrealisme naar de Verenigde Staten, waar Man Ray, Duchamp en andere kunstenaars worden opgewacht door scherpzinnige verzamelaars en vindingrijke jonge kunstenaars. De naoorlogse periode ziet dan ook de artistieke decors van Parijs naar New York verplaatsen, waar een nieuwe geschiedenis op het punt staat te beginnen. De nieuwe studies baseren zich op het psychisch automatisme, op het onvoorwaardelijke opdoemen van het onderdrukte en op de vrijheid van de surrealistische meesters.

Surrealist Posters and Magazines
Surrealistische Manifeste und Zeitschriften
Affiches et revues surréalistes
Surrealistische manifesten en tijdschriften

1900
Cover of the "Dictionnaire Abrégé du Surréalisme"
Umschlag "Dictionnaire abrégé du surréalisme"
Couverture du « Dictionnaire abrégé du Surréalisme »
Omslag van de "Dictionnaire abrégé du surréalisme"

1924
Cover of first edition of Dadaist magazine "La revolution surrealiste" edited by Tristan Tzara in Paris
Umschlag der Nr.1. der Dada-Zeitschrift "La revolution surreaiste", herausgegeben von Tristan Tzara in Paris
Couverture du numero 1 du journal dadaiste « La revolution surrealiste » editee par Tristan Tzara a Paris
Omslag van het eerste nummer van het dadaïstische tijdschrift "La revolution surrealiste", verzorgd door Tristan Tzara te Parijs
Private Collection / Privatsammlung / Collection privée / Privécollectie

| 1900 | 1910 | 1915 | 1920 | 1925 |

1922
Cover of first edition of Dadaist magazine "Le Coeur à barbe" edited by Tristan Tzara in Paris
Umschlag der Nr.1. der Dada-Zeitschrift "Le Coeur à barbe", herausgegeben von Tristan Tzara in Paris
Couverture du 1er numéro de la revue dadaïste « Le Cœur à barbe »
Omslag van het eerste nummer van het dadaïstische tijdschrift "Le Coeur à barbe", verzorgd door Tristan Tzara te Parijs
Private Collection / Privatsammlung / Collection privée / Privécollectie

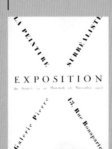

1925
Catalogue for the last collective exhibition of surrealist painting at the Galerie Pierre, 1925: De Chirico, Max Ernst, Paul Klee, A. Masson, Miró, Picasso, Man Ray, Pierre Roy
Katalog der letzten Gemeinschaftsausstellung surrealistischer Malerei in der Galerie Pierre, 1925: De Chirico, Max Ernst, Paul Klee, A. Masson, Miró, Picasso, Man Ray, Pierre Roy
Catalogue pour la dernière exposition collective de peinture surréaliste à la Galerie Pierre, 1925 : De Chirico, Max Ernst, Paul Klee, A. Masson, Miró, Picasso, Man Ray, Pierre Roy
Catalogus voor de laatste collectieve tentoonstelling van de surrealistische schilderkunst bij de Galerie Pierre, 1925: De Chirico, Max Ernst, Paul Klee, A. Masson, Miró, Picasso, Man Ray, Pierre Roy

1935
Cover of "Surrealismus"
Umschlag "Surrealismus"
Couverture « Surrealismus »
Omslag van de "Surrealismus"
Private Collection / Privatsammlung /
Collection privée / Privécollectie

A PARTIR DU 17 JANVIER 1938

EXPOSITION

INTERNATIONALE

DU

SURRÉALISME

GALERIE BEAUX-ARTS, 140 F S HONORÉ

1938
Poster for the Exposition International
Surrealism at the Galerie Beaux Arts in Paris
Plakat der Internationalen Surrealistischen
Ausstellung in der Galerie Beaux Arts in Paris
Affiche de l'Exposition Internationale du
Surréalisme à la Galerie Beaux-Arts, Paris
Manifest van de Internationale Expositie van
het Surrealisme bij de Galerie des Beaux Arts
in Parijs
Private Collection / Privatsammlung /
Collection privée / Privécollectie

1948
First page of "Neon", a surrealist
magazine
Titelblatt der surrealistischen
Zeitschrift "Neon"
La une de « Néon », revue surréaliste
Eerste pagina van "Neon",
surrealistisch tijdschrift
Private Collection / Privatsammlung /
Collection privée / Privécollectie

| 1930 | 1935 | 1940 | 1945 | 1950 |

INTE
PICTURES
SCULPTURE
OBJECTS
LECTURES
FILMS
SUR
EXH
NEW BURLINGTON GALLERIES
BURLINGTON GARDENS
OPENING CEREMONY 3 p.m., THURSDAY, JUNE 11th, 1936
PRESS VIEW 10 a.m.
EXHIBITION OPEN JUNE 12th-JULY 4th, 10-5
ADMISSION 1/3 INCLUDING SATURDAYS

1936
Invitation to the International Surrealist Exhibition, 11/06/1936 at the New Burlington Galleries, London
Einladung zur Internationalen Surrealistischen Ausstellung am 11/06/1936 in der Galerie New Burlington
Invitation pour International Surrealist Exhibition à New Burlington Galleries le 11/06/1936
Uitnodiging voor de Internationale Surrealistische Tentoonstelling, op 11/06/1936 bij de New Burlington Galleries
Bibliothèque Jacques Doucet, Paris

1938
Max Ernst
Cover of the magazine
"Minotaure" n°11
Max Ernst, Umschlag der
Zeitschrift "Minotaure" Nr.11
Max Ernst, couverture de la
revue « Minotaure », n°11
Max Ernst, omslag voor het
tijdschrift "Minotaure", nr. 11
Private Collection /
Privatsammlung / Collection
privée / Privécollectie

Max Ernst
(Brühl 1891 - Paris 1976)
The king plays with the queen, bronze
Der König spielt mit der Königin, Bronze
Le Roi jouant avec la Reine, bronze
De koning speelt met de koningin, brons
1944 (1954)
60 x 47 x 20 cm / 23.6 x 18.5 x 7.8 in.
Museum of Modern Art, New York

▶ **Max Ernst**
(Brühl 1891 - Paris 1976)
Apres moi le sommeil, oil on canvas
Nach mir der Schlaf, Öl auf Leinwand
Après moi le sommeil, huile sur toile
Après moi le sommeil, olieverf op doek
1958
130 x 89 cm / 51.1 x 35 in.
Centre Georges Pompidou, Musée National d'Art Moderne, Paris

Victor Brauner
(Piatra Neamt 1903 - Paris 1966)
Prelude to civilisation, encaustic and pen and ink on masonite
Präludium für die Zivilisation, Enkaustik, Feder und Tinte auf Hartfaserplatte
Prélude à une civilisation, encaustique, plume et encre sur masonite
Prelude op de civilisatie, wasschildering, pen en inkt op masoniet
c. 1963
129,5 x 202,5 cm / 50.9 x 79.5 x 1.9 in.
Metropolitan Museum of Art, New York

▶ **Joseph Cornell**
(Nyack, New York 1903 - New York 1972)
Ideas are like stars: you will not succeed in touching them with your hand, assemblage painted
and stained wood, glass, shells, driftwood and paper
Die Ideale sind wie Sterne: Du wirst diese, mit deinen Händen, nie berühren können,
Zusammensetzung aus Holz mit Beizmittel und Lack, Glas, Muschel, andere Materialien
Les idéaux sont comme les étoiles : on ne réussira jamais à les toucher avec ses mains,
assemblage de bois avec mordant et vernis, verre, coquillages et matériaux divers
Idealen zijn als sterren: het lukt je nooit om ze met je handen aan te raken, assemblage van
hout, bijtmiddel en verf, glas, schelpen, diverse materialen
1957-1958
44,2 x 32,7 x 8,9 cm / 17.4 x 12.8 x 3.5 in.
Smithsonian American Art Museum, Washington DC

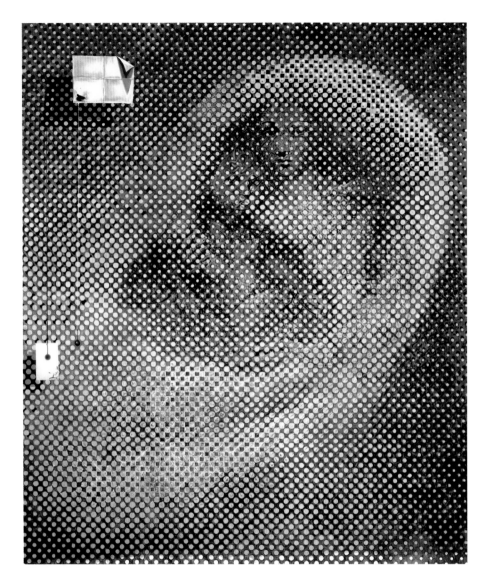

Salvador Dalí
(Figueres 1904 - 1989)
Madonna
Oil on canvas
Öl auf Leinwand
Huile sur toile
Olieverf op doek
1958
225,7 x 191,1 cm / 88.8 x 75.2 in.
Metropolitan Museum of Art, New York

▶ **Salvador Dalí**
(Figueres 1904 - 1989)
Crucifixion (Corpus Hypercubus), oil on canvas
Kreuzigung (Corpus Hypercubus), Öl auf Leinwand
Crucifixion (Corpus Hypercubus), huile sur toile
Kruisiging (Corpus Hypercubus), olieverf op doek
1954
194,5 x 124 cm / 76,5 x 48,8 in.
Metropolitan Museum of Art, New York

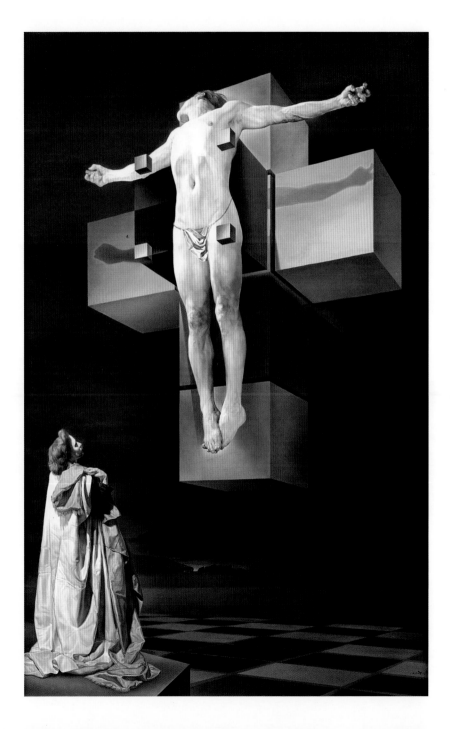

Joan Miró
(Barcelona 1893 - Palma de Mallorca 1983)
Mural painting, oil on canvas
Wandmalerei, Öl auf Leinwand
Peinture murale, huile sur toile
Muurschildering, olieverf op doek
1950-1951
188,8 x 593,8 cm / 74.3 x 233.7 in.
Museum of Modern Art, New York

▶ **Joan Miró**
(Barcelona 1893 - Palma de Mallorca 1983)
Wall of the sun, polychrome ceramic
Mauer der Sonne, mehrfarbige Keramik
Mur du Soleil, plaques de céramique polychrome émaillée
Muur van de zon, polychroom keramiek
1958
Palais de l'Unesco, Paris

◀ **Jean (Hans) Arp**
(Strasbourg 1887 - Basel 1966)
Mural reliefs, wooden shapes mounted on a wall
Wandreliefs, Verschiedena Holzformen ausgeschnitten und aufgetragen auf Wand
Reliefs muraux, diverses formes de bois découpées et montées sur un mur
Wandreliëfs, verschillende houten vormen, op een wand gemonteerd
1954-1957
Palais de l'Unesco, Paris

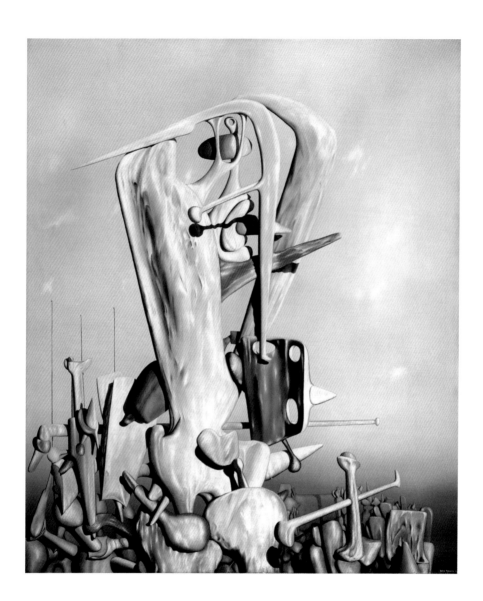

Yves Tanguy
(Paris 1900 - Woodbury, CT., 1955)
My life, black and white, oil on canvas
Mein Leben, Schwarz-Weiß, Öl auf Leinwand
Ma vie, noir et blanc, huile sur toile
Mijn leven, Zwart en Wit, olieverf op doek
1944
99 x 81,3 cm / 38.9 x 32 in.
Metropolitan Museum of Art, New York

▶ **Yves Tanguy**
(Paris 1900 - Woodbury, CT., 1955)
Imaginary number, oil on canvas
Imaginäre Zahlen, Öl auf Leinwand
Nombres imaginaires, huile sur toile
Imaginair nummer, olieverf op doek
1954
99 x 80 cm / 38.9 x 31.4 in.
Museo Thyssen-Bornemisza, Madrid

André Masson
(Balagny-sur-Thérain 1896 - Paris 1987)
The animal's den, oil on canvas
Die Höhle, Öl auf Leinwand
Le Terrier, huile sur toile
De schuilplaats, olieverf op doek
1946
84 x 102 cm / 33 x 40.1 in.
Musée Cantini, Marseille

◀ **André Masson**
(Balagny-sur-Thérain 1896 - Paris 1987)
Bird in the Camargue, oil on canvas
Vogel über die Camargue, Öl auf Leinwand
Oiseau au-dessus de la Camargue, huile sur toile
Vogel op Camargue, olieverf op doek
1949
65 x 49,5 cm / 25.5 x 19.4 in.
Hamburger Kunsthalle, Hamburg

René Magritte
(Lessen 1898 - Brussel 1967)
The beautiful prisoner, oil on canvas
Die schöne Gefangene, Öl auf Leinwand
La Belle Prisonnière, huile sur toile
De mooie gevangene (La belle captive), olieverf op doek
1950
30 x 40 cm / 11.8 x 15.7 in.
Private Collection / Privatsammlung / Collection privée / Privécollectie

▶ **René Magritte**
(Lessen 1898 - Brussel 1967)
Le grand style, oil on canvas
Großer Stil (Le grand style), Öl auf Leinwand
Le Grand Style, huile sur toile
Le grand style, olieverf op doek
1951
80 x 60 cm / 31.4 x 23.6 in.
The Menil Collection, Houston

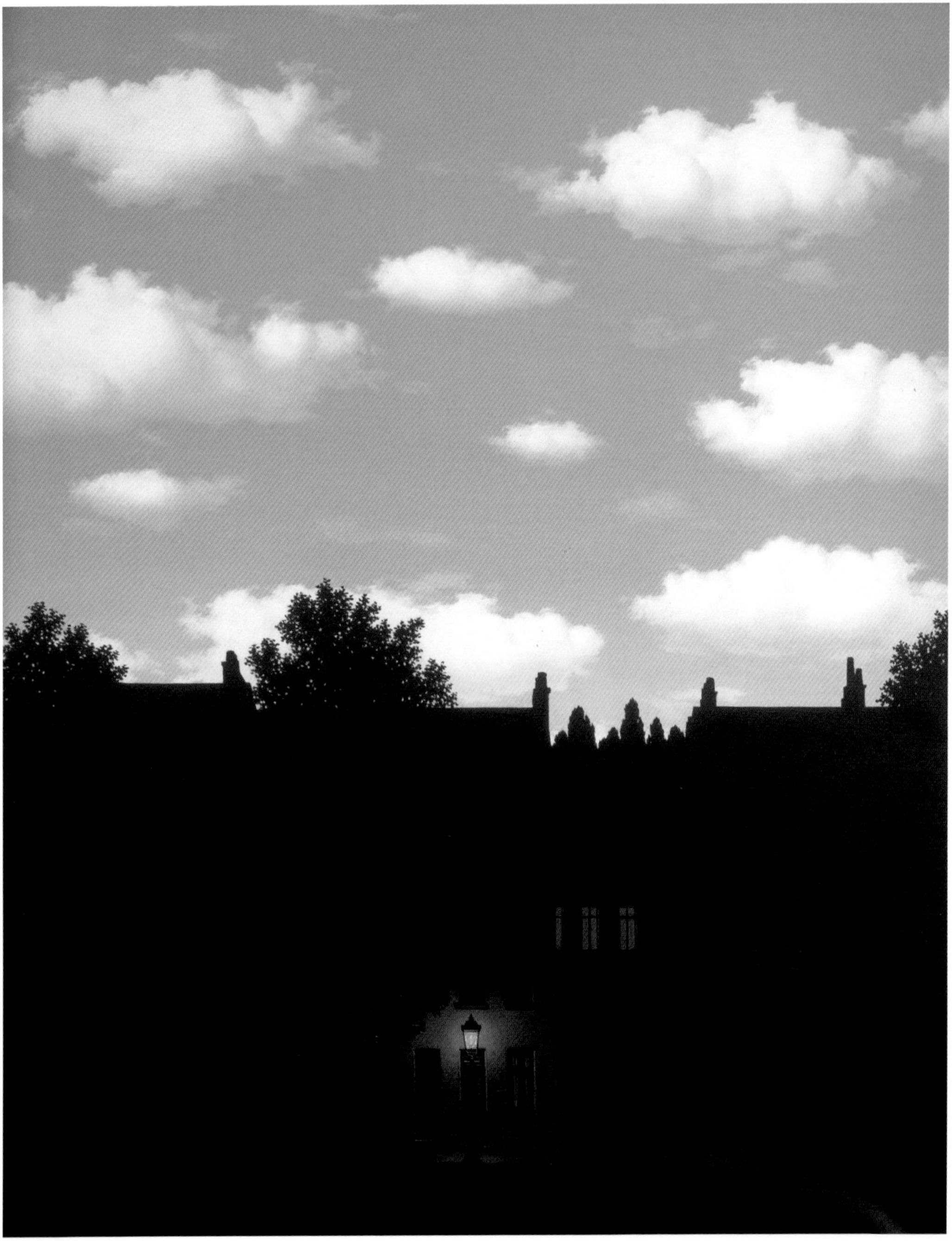

René Magritte
(Lessen 1898 - Brussel 1967)
Galconde
Oil on canvas
Öl auf Leinwand
Huile sur toile
Olieverf op doek
1953
80,7 x 100,6 cm / 31.7 x 39.6 in.
The Menil Collection, Houston

◀ **René Magritte**
(Lessen 1898 - Brussel 1967)
The Empire of Light, oil on canvas
Das Reich der Lichter, Öl auf Leinwand
L'Empire des lumières, huile sur toile
Het rijk der lichten, olieverf op doek
1952
100 x 80 cm / 39.3 x 31.4 in.
Private Collection / Privatsammlung / Collection privée / Privécollectie

René Magritte
(Lessen 1898 - Brussel 1967)
The masterpiece or the mysteries of the horizon, oil on canvas
Das Meisterwerk oder die Mysterien des Horizonts, Öl auf Leinwand
Le Chef-d'œuvre, ou les mystères de l'horizon, huile sur toile
Het meesterwerk of de geheimen van de horizon, olieverf op doek
1955
50 x 65 cm / 19.6 x 25.5 in.
Frederick Weisman Company, Los Angeles

▶ **René Magritte**
(Lessen 1898 - Brussel 1967)
Le bouquet tout fait, oil on canvas
Das vollendete Bukett, Öl auf Leinwand
Le Bouquet tout fait, huile sur toile
Le bouquet tout fait, olieverf op doek
1956
60 x 50 cm / 23.6 x 19.6 in.
Private Collection / Privatsammlung / Collection privée / Privécollectie

René Magritte
(Lessen 1898 - Brussel 1967)
The listening room, oil on canvas
Das Zimmer des Lauschens, Öl auf Leinwand
La chambre d'écoute, huile sur toile
De luisterkamer (La chambre d'écoute), olieverf op doek
1958
38 x 46 cm / 14.9 x 18.1 in.
Private Collection / Privatsammlung / Collection privée / Privécollectie

René Magritte
(Lessen 1898 - Brussel 1967)
The battle of the Argonne, oil on canvas
Die Schlacht von Argonne, Öl auf Leinwand
La bataille de l'Argonne, huile sur toile
De slag in de Argonne, olieverf op doek
1959
50 x 61 cm / 19.6 x 24 in.
Private Collection / Privatsammlung / Collection privée / Privécollectie

René Magritte
(Lessen 1898 - Brussel 1967)
The castle in the Pyrenees, oil on canvas
Das Schloss in den Pyrenäen, Öl auf Leinwand
La château des Pyrénées, huile sur toile
Het kasteel van de Pyreneeën, olieverf op doek
1959
200,3 x 130,3 cm / 78.8 x 51.2 in.
Israel Museum, Jerusalem

René Magritte
(Lessen 1898 - Brussel 1967)
La ricerche de l'absolu, gouache on paper
Auf der Suche nach dem Absoluten, Gouache auf Papier
La recherche de l'absolu, gouache sur papier
Het zoeken naar het absolute, gouache op papier
1964
55 x 36 cm / 21.6 x 14.1 in.
Private Collection / Privatsammlung / Collection privée / Privécollectie

Pablo Picasso
(Málaga 1881 - Mougins 1973)
Goat, skull and bottle, assemblage in painted bronze and other materials
Ziege, Schädel und Flasche, Assemblage aus bemalter Bronze, anderen Elementen und Materialien
Crâne de chèvre, bouteille et bougie, assemblage de bronze peint et d'autres éléments et matériaux
Geitenschedel en fles (Vallauris), assemblage van beschilderd brons en andere elementen en materialen
1954
78,8 x 95,3x54,5 cm / 31 x 37.5 x 21.4 in.
Museum of Modern Art, New York

▶ **Pablo Picasso**
(Málaga 1881 - Mougins 1973)
Faun and starry night, oil on canvas
Faunus und Sternennacht, Öl auf Leinwand
Faune et nuit étoilée, huile sur toile
Faun en sterrennacht, olieverf op doek
1955
73,7 x 92,7 cm / 29 x 36.4 in.
Metropolitan Museum of Art, New York

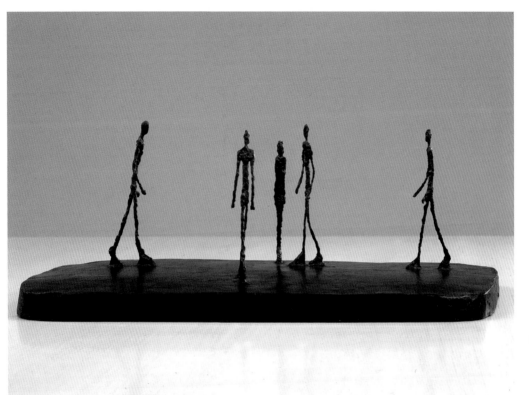

Alberto Giacometti
(Borgonovo di Stampa 1901 - Chur 1966)
La piazza II, bronze
Der Platz II, Bronze
La place II, bronze
Het plein II, brons
1948-1949
23 x 63,5 x 43,5 cm / 9 x 24.9 x 17.1 in.
Nationalgalerie, Museum Berggruen, Staatliche Museen zu Berlin, Berlin

◄ **Alberto Giacometti**
(Borgonovo di Stampa 1901 - Chur 1966)
Three men walking (II), bronze
Drei schreitende Männer (II), Bronze
Trois hommes qui marchent (II), bronze
Drie wandelende mannen (II), brons
1949
76,5 x 33 x 32,4 cm / 30.1 x 12.9 x 12.7 in.
Metropolitan Museum of Art, New York

Alberto Giacometti
(Borgonovo di Stampa 1901 -
Chur 1966)
Portrait of Diego, oil on canvas
Porträt von Diego, Öl auf Leinwand
Portrait de Diego, huile sur toile
Portret van Diego, olieverf op doek
c.1953
Collection Maeght, Paris

◄ **Alberto Giacometti**
(Borgonovo di Stampa 1901 -
Chur 1966)
Cart, bronze
Der Wagen, Bronze
Char, bronze peint sur un support
en bois
Wagen, brons
1950
144,8 x 65,8 x 66,2 cm /
57 x 25.9 x 26 in.
Museum of Modern Art, New York

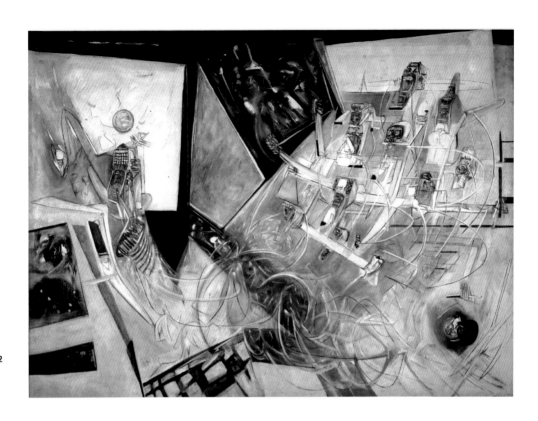

Roberto Sebastian Matta
(Santiago de Chile 1911 - Civitavecchia 2002)
Contra Vosotros Asesinos de Palomas, oil on canvas
Gegen euch Taubentöter, Öl auf Leinwand
Contra vosotros, asesinos de palomas, huile sur toile
Contra Vosotros Asesinos de Palomas, olieverf op doek
1950
200 x 271 cm / 78.7 x 106.6 in.
Musée Cantini, Marseille

Roberto Sebastian Matta
(Santiago de Chile 1911 - Civitavecchia 2002)
La Vie Est Touchée
Oil on canvas
Öl auf Leinwand
Huile sur toile
Olieverf op doek
1957
144,8 x 204,5 x 2,2 cm / 57 x 80.5 x 0.8 in.
Yale University Art Gallery, New Haven

Roberto Sebastian Matta
(Santiago de Chile 1911 - Civitavecchia 2002)
L'Honni Aveuglant: L'honni aveuglant
Oil on canvas
Öl auf Leinwand
Huile sur toile
Olieverf op doek
1966
200 x 195 cm / 78.7 x 76.7 in.
Museo Thyssen-Bornemisza, Madrid

Roberto Sebastian Matta
(Santiago de Chile 1911 - Civitavecchia 2002)
L'Honni Aveuglant: Le où à marée haute
Oil on canvas
Öl auf Leinwand
Huile sur toile
Olieverf op doek
1966
202 x 195 cm / 79.5 x 76.7 in.
Museo Thyssen-Bornemisza, Madrid

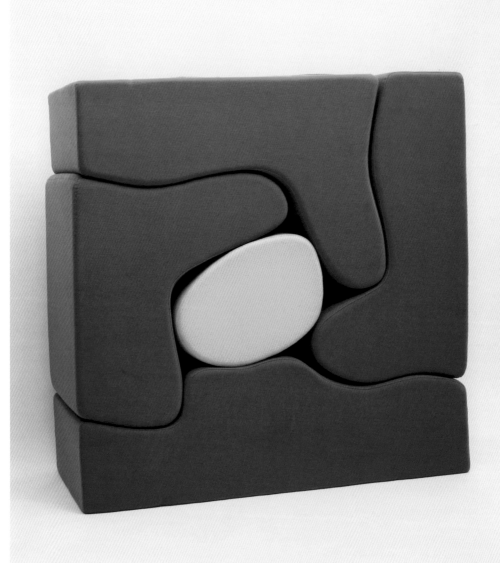

Roberto Sebastian Matta
(Santiago de Chile 1911 - Civitavecchia 2002)
Malitte lounge furniture and detail, expanded polyurethane and wool
Wohnzimmereinrichtung Malitte und detail, Polyurethan-Schaum und Wolle
Mobilier de salon Malitte, et détail, polyuréthane expansé et laine
Malitte, lounge meubel en détail, polyurethaan schuim en wol
1966
160 x 160 x 63,5 cm / 62.9 x 62.9 x 24.9 in.
Museum of Modern Art, New York

Wilfredo Lam
(Sagua la Grande, Cuba 1902 - Paris 1982)
The wedding, oil on canvas
Die Flitterwochen, Öl auf Leinwand
Les Noces, huile sur toile
De bruiloft, olieverf op doek
1947
215 x 197 cm / 84.6 x 77.5 in.
Nationalgalerie, Museum Berggruen, Staatliche Museen zu Berlin, Berlin

Barbara Hepworth
(Wakefield 1903 - St Ives 1975)
Pierced Form (Toledo), mahogany and strings
Durchbohrte Form, Holz und Schnur
Forme perforée – (Tolède), bois et corde
Doorstoken vorm, (Toledo), hout en koord
1957
h. 90 cm / 35.4 in.
Private Collection / Privatsammlung /
Collection privée / Privécollectie

▶ **Henry Moore**
(Castleford 1898 - Much Hadham 1986)
Head of an animal, plaster
Tierkopf, Gips
Tête d'animal, plâtre
Kop van een dier, gips
1952
h. 30,5 cm / 12 in.
Tate Gallery, London

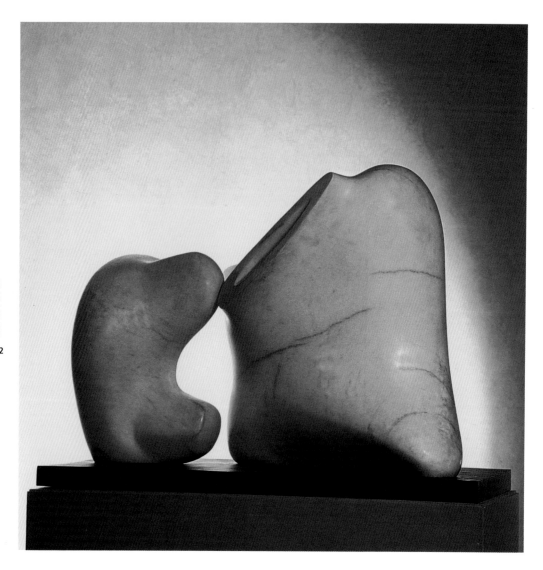

Henry Moore
(Castleford 1898 - Much Hadham 1986)
Mother and son, pink aurora marble
Mutter und Sohn, Morgenrosa Marmor
Mère et fils, marbre rose
Moeder en zoon, Rose Aurora marmer
1966
h.130 cm / 51.1 in.
Private Collection / Privatsammlung /
Collection privée / Privécollectie

▶ **Henry Moore**
(Castleford 1898 - Much Hadham 1986)
Great arch, fibre-glass
Der Bogen, Glasfaser
Grand arc, fibre de verre
Grote boog, glasfiber
1963-1971
h. 610 cm / 240.1 in.
Bartholomew Country Public, Columbus (Indiana)

Chronology
Chronologie

1916

▌ In Zürich the international Dada movement is launched in response to the catastrophe of the First World War, and to the provocation of the Futurists and the Expressionists. The "farce of nothing" takes place at the Café Voltaire.

▌ In Reaktion auf die Katastrofen des ersten Weltkriegs und auch auf die Provokationen des Futurismus und Expressionismus wird in Zürich die internationale Dadabewegung geboren. Im Kabarett Voltaire wird die "Die Farce des Nichts" vorgestellt.

▌ Le mouvement du dadaïsme, à vocation internationale, naît à Zurich, en réaction à la catastrophe de la Première Guerre mondiale, mais aussi aux provocations du futurisme et de l'expressionnisme. On met en scène, au Cabaret Voltaire, « la farce du néant ».

▌ In Zürich ontstaat de internationale beweging van het dadaïsme. Dada is niet alleen een antwoord op de catastrofe van de Eerste Wereldoorlog, maar ook op provocaties van het futurisme en expressionisme. In café Voltaire wordt "De klucht van het niets" opgevoerd.

1917

▌ Marcel Duchamp comes up with the first ready-made, and he begins experimenting with arbitrariness, homophonic word games, "useless machines" and all possible stratagems for combining chance and choice in his "works of art without an artist". In Italy the Metaphysical movement is born. Giorgio De Chirico paints his "unquiet Muses".

▌ Die ersten Ready-mades von Marcel Duchamp tauchen auf. Zugleich experimentiert er mit der Zweideutigkeit, mit homophonen Wortspielen, mit den "unnötigen Maschinen" und mit allen Mitteln die eine Kombination von Zufall und Auswahl, Willkürlichkeit und Wille in seinen "Kunstwerken ohne Künstler" ermöglichen. In Italien wird die Bewegung der Methaphysik offiziell geboren. Giorgio De Chirico malt seine "Beunruhigenden Musen".

▌ Naissance des premiers ready-made de Marcel Duchamp. L'artiste expérimente en art les méthodes de l'arbitraire, des jeux de mots homophones, des « machines inutiles » et de tous les stratagèmes possibles pour combiner choix, hasard, arbitraire et volonté, dans ses « œuvres d'art sans artiste ». Naissance officielle du mouvement de la peinture métaphysique en Italie. Giorgio De Chirico peint ses *Muses inquiétantes*.

▌ Marcel Duchamp maakt zijn eerste ready-made's. De kunstenaar experimenteert met de methode van de willekeur, woordspelletjes met gelijk klinkende woorden (homofonie) en creëert 'onbruikbare machines'. Hij maakt in zijn 'kunstwerken zonder kunstenaar' gebruik van alle mogelijke strategieën om toeval en keuze, willekeur en wil, te combineren. In Italië ontstaat officieel de Metafysische schilderkunst. Giorgio De Chirico schildert "De verontruste Muzen".

1920

▌ The First International Dada Fair is held in Berlin: the politicisation of the artistic process leads to the emergence of photomontage as a new artistic medium that is as effective as it is devastating.

▌ In Berlin findet die Dada-Messe statt: Die Politisierung künstlerischer Praktiken führt zur Fotomontage als neues Kunstmedium, wirksam und zugleich venichtend.

▌ Organisation de la « foire Dada » : la politisation des pratiques artistiques conduit à la création du photomontage comme support artistique nouveau – aussi efficace que dévastateur.

▌ In Berlijn wordt de *Dada-Messe* gehouden: de politisering van kunstuitingen maakt de fotomontage, een even efficiënt als verwoestend nieuw artistiek medium, noodzakelijk.

1921 ▮ André Breton encounters Sigmund Freud in Vienna.

▮ In Wien findet das Treffen zwischen Sigmund Freud und André Breton statt.

▮ Sigmund Freud rencontre André Breton à Vienne.

▮ In Wenen vindt de ontmoeting plaats tussen Sigmund Freud en André Breton.

1922 ▮ In Paris the Dadaist poet Tristan Tzara recites the funeral oration of Dada. But although Dada dies, its creative and uninhibited spirit – provocative, caustic, explosive – is destined to flow directly into the nascent surrealist movement.Hans Prinzhorn publishes *The Artistry of the Mentally Ill*: it prompts Max Ernst to explore "the art of psychopathic persons".

▮ In Paris stellt der Dada-Dichter Tristan Tzara die Grabrede dar. Obwohl Dada stirbt, wird seine kreative, hemmungslose, provokante, bissige, explosive Seele in die bevorstehenden Geburt des Surrealismus übergehen. Hans Prinzhorn veröffentlicht *Die Bildnerei der Geisteskranken*: Basierend auf den Werken von Max Ernst wird die "Kunst der Psychopaten" erforscht

▮ À Paris, le poète dadaïste Tristan Tzara prononce l'oraison funèbre de Dada. Mais si Dada est mort, son esprit créatif et désinhibé, provocateur, caustique et explosif est destiné à se transférer au mouvement surréaliste dont la naissance est imminente. Le Dr Hans Prinzhorn publie *La Créativité plastique des malades mentaux* : de cette théorie naît chez Max Ernst l'idée d'explorer et d'exploiter dans ses œuvres « l'art des psychopathes ».

▮ In Parijs draagt de dadaïst Tristan Tzara de grafrede van Dada voor. Dada sterft, maar haar geest, creatief en vrijgevochten, provocerend, sarcastisch en explosief, blijft doorstromen in de opkomende surrealistische beweging. Hans Prinzhorn publiceert *Bildnerei der Geisteskranken*: vanuit deze optiek worden in de kunst van Max Ernst de symptomen van 'psychopathologische kunst' onderzocht.

1924 ▮ André Breton publishes the First Manifesto of Surrealism and the first number of *La Révolution Surréaliste*, laying down the guiding principles for the new group. Alberto Savinio begins to paint, while continuing his literary activity on behalf of surrealism.

▮ André Breton veröffentlicht das Erste Manifest des Surrealismus und die erste Ausgabe der Zeitschrift "la Révolution Surréaliste", wo sich die Wurzeln der Forschung von dem sich bildenden Surrealismus befinden. Alberto Savinio widmet sich neben seiner literarischen Tätigkeit,die dem Surrealismus nahe steht, auch der Malerei.

▮ André Breton publie le premier *Manifeste du surréalisme* et le premier numéro d'une revue – *La Révolution surréaliste* – où sont établis les principes essentiels des recherches du groupe naissant. À côté de recherches littéraires proches des milieux surréalistes, Alberto Savinio (de son vrai nom Andrea De Chirico, frère de Giorgio) se consacre aussi à la peinture.

▮ André Breton publiceert het 'Eerste Manifest van het Surrealisme'. In het eerste nummer van 'De Surrealistische Revolutie' worden de grondslagen van de opkomende surrealistische beweging bekrachtigd. Alberto Savinio wijdt zich, naast zijn onderzoek naar literatuur die verwant is aan het surrealisme, aan de schilderkunst.

1927 ∎ The Belgian painter René Magritte joins the Surrealists in Paris. He begins to play with the contents of advertising and with the ambiguities of language and representation. André Breton, Louis Aragon and Paul Éluard formally join the Communist Party. The Spanish artist Salvador Dalí travels for the first time to Paris where he meets Picasso. Together with his friend Mirò he comes into contact with the French Surrealists.

∎ Der Belgier René Magritte vereint sich mit den Surrealisten von Paris. Seine Forschung spielt mit den öffentlichen Formen und der Zweideutigkeit der Sprachen und Darstellungen. André Breton, Louis Aragon, Paul Éluard treten offiziell dem Kommunismus bei. Der Spanier Salvador Dalí reist zum ersten Mal nach Paris, wo er Picasso trifft. Zusammen mit seinem Freund Mirò kommt er mit den französischen Surrealisten in Kontakt.

∎ Le Belge René Magritte rejoint les surréalistes à Paris. Ses recherches jouent sur les formes et les usages de la publicité, sur les ambiguïtés du langage et de la représentation. André Breton, Louis Aragon et Paul Éluard (de son vrai nom Eugène Grindel) adhèrent officiellement au communisme. L'Espagnol Salvador Dalí se rend pour la première fois à Paris où il rencontre Picasso. Avec son ami Joan Miró, il entre lui aussi en contact avec les surréalistes français.

∎ De Belg René Magritte sluit zich aan bij de surrealisten in Parijs. In zijn werk speelt hij met publiciteit en de ambiguïteit van taal en beeldvormen. André Breton, Louis Aragon en Paul Éluard worden lid van de Communistische Partij. De Spanjaard Salvador Dalí gaat voor het eerst naar Parijs, waar hij Picasso ontmoet. Samen met zijn vriend Mirò komt hij in contact met de Franse surrealisten.

1929 ∎ In his second Surrealist Manifesto, André Breton links the moral rebellion fermented by the psychoanalytic approach of Freud to the social rebellion brought about by the study of Marx. Artists react in different ways and a split develops between those who are in favour of, and those who are against (or indifferent to), Communism, the dictatorship of the Proletariat, Trotsky's Permanent Revolution and the Third International.

∎ Im Zweiten Manifest des Surrealismus verbindet André Breton die moralische Rebellion, die vom psychoanalytischen Denken von Freud getrieben wird, mit der sozialen Revolution von Marx. Die Künstler reagieren auf den Kommunismus, die Diktatur des Proletariats, sowie auf die Permanente Revolution von Trotzki und der Dritten Internationale nauf verschiedenste Weise. Somit spalten sie sich in jene die dafür, dagegen oder unparteiisch sind.

∎ Dans un second *Manifeste* surréaliste, André Breton unit la révolte morale induite par la théorie psychanalytique de Freud à la révolte sociale découlant des analyses de Marx. Les membres du groupe réagissent de façons différentes : une scission se produit entre les partisans, les adversaires et/ou les indifférents vis-à-vis du communisme et de la « dictature du prolétariat », de la « révolution permanente » prônée par Léon Trotski et de la IIIe Internationale.

∎ In een tweede Surrealistisch Manifest verbindt André Breton, onder invloed van Freud's psychoanalyse, de opstand van de moraal met de sociale opstand uit de analyse van Marx. De kunstenaars reageren verschillend. Er ontstaat een breuk tussen voorstanders en tegenstanders, of degenen die onverschillig staan tegenover het communisme, de dictatuur van het proletariaat, Trotsky's Permanente Revolutie en de Derde Internationale.

1930

▮ Georges Bataille reviews *L'art primitif*, bringing to light a disagreement within the surrealism movement in the attitudes of various artists towards primitive modes of expression. The first surrealist exhibition in the United States.

▮ Georges Bataille rezensiert die *Primitive Kunst* und betont die Zerrissenheit zwischen Künstlern und primitiver Kunst innerhalb des Surrealismus. Erste surrealistische Ausstellung in den Vereinigten Staaten.

▮ Georges Bataille écrit « *L'art primitif* », recension qui met en évidence un schisme au sein du surréalisme, dans le rapport que les divers artistes entretiennent avec cet art et ses représentations. Première exposition surréaliste aux États-Unis.

▮ Georges Bataille publiceert het artikel '*L'art primitif*'. Binnen het surrealisme is een tweedeling ontstaan in de relatie die kunstenaars met primitieve kunst hebben. De eerste surrealistische tentoonstelling in de Verenigde Staten.

1931

▮ Alberto Giacometti, Salvador Dalí and André Breton publish essays on "the object in its symbolic function" in the journal *Le Surréalisme au service de la révolution*. The movement extends the aesthetics of fetishism and fantasy to the sphere of artistic production.

▮ Alberto Giacometti, Salvador Dalí und André Breton veröffentlichen Texte über "Objekte mit symbolischer Funktion"in ihre Zeitschrift "Le Surréalisme au service de la révolution". Die Bewegung weitet die Fantasie und Fetischästetik bis in die künstlerische Produktion aus.

▮ Alberto Giacometti, Salvador Dalí et André Breton publient des textes sur « l'objet à fonctionnement symbolique » dans la revue *Le Surréalisme au service de la révolution*. Les théoriciens du mouvement étendent alors l'esthétique du fétichisme et de la bizarrerie à l'univers de la production artistique.

▮ Alberto Giacometti, Salvador Dalí en André Breton publiceren in het tijdschrift "*Le Surréalisme au service de la révolution*" een artikel over de symbolische functie van het voorwerp. De surrealisten introduceren de esthetiek van het fetisjisme en de fantasie in de kunstwereld.

1934

▮ Henry Moore, with his stone sculptures made by "direct carving", offers an original symbiosis between the figurative and the abstract, between surrealism and constructivism. Together with his friend Barbara Hepworth, Moore joins the group Unit One, and in the "pure search for form" concentrates on "following the trail of the psyche", taking his lead from the surrealists.

▮ Henry Moore stellt mit seinen Steinskulpturen, die mit "direktem Schnitt" hergestellt wurden, eine originelle Symbiose zwischen Darstellung und Abstraktion, sowie Surrealismus und Konstruktivismus dar. Moore kommt mitder Gruppe Unit One in Kontakt, an der auch seine Freundin Barbara Hepworth teilnimmt. Auf der „reinen Suche nach der Form "konzentriert man sich nach surrealistischem Beispiel auf die "Spurder Psyche".

▮ Avec ses sculptures en pierre réalisées en « taille directe », Henry Moore propose une symbiose originale entre figuration et abstraction, entre surréalisme et constructivisme. Moore entre en contact avec le groupe Unit One auquel participe son amie Barbara Hepworth : dans sa « recherche pure de la forme », ce groupe se concentre sur l'objectif de « suivre les traces de la psyché » selon les exemples du surréalisme.

▮ Henry Moore maakt met zijn 'direct carving' – een techniek waarbij direct in de steen wordt gehakt – beelden waarin een originele symbiose te zien is tussen figuratie en abstractie, surrealisme en constructivisme. Moore komt in contact met de groep *Unit One*, waar ook zijn vriendin Barbara Hepworth aan deelneemt. In een 'oprecht zoeken naar de vorm' willen de kunstenaars in navolging van het surrealisme 'de sporen van de psyche volgen'.

1936	▮ Major exhibition of Surrealist objects in Paris.	▮ Große Ausstellung von surrealistischen Gegenständen in Paris.	▮ Grande exposition d'objets surréalistes à Paris.	▮ Grote tentoonstelling in Parijs met surrealistische objecten.
1938	▮ In Mexico, Breton visits Trotsky, Rivera and Frida Kahlo.	▮ Breton besucht Trockij, Rivera und Frida Kahlo in Mexico.	▮ À Mexico, Breton rend visite à Trotski, Diego Rivera et Frida Kahlo.	▮ Breton bezoekt in Mexico Trotsky, Rivera en Frida Kahlo.
1940	▮ After the Nazi occupation of France, Salvador Dalí takes refuge in the United States, where his painting and his "paranoiac and critical method" achieve great fame and worldly success.	▮ Mit der Nazi-Besetzung in Frankreich flüchtet Salvador Dalí in die Vereinigten Staaten, wo seine Forschung und seine "kritische und paranoide Methode" großen Erfolg und Annerkennung feiert.	▮ Suite à l'occupation de la France par les Allemands, Salvador Dalí se réfugie aux États-Unis, où ses recherches et sa fameuse « méthode paranoïaque-critique » lui valent de grands succès mondains… et financiers.	▮ Als Frankrijk door de nazi's is bezet, vlucht Salvador Dalí naar de Verenigde Staten. Hij wordt beroemd met zijn werk en zijn 'paranoïde en kritische methode' en oogst veel succes in de mondaine wereld.
1942	▮ The Second World War compels many Surrealists to emigrate to the United States. Among these are Breton, Ernst, Masson, Matta and Lam. Surrealism influences the United States, while the avant-garde in both the new and the old world borrow ideas from the masters of Surrealism in order to create new artistic languages.	▮ Der Ausbruch des Zweiten Weltkriegs zwingt viele Surrealisten zum Exil in die Vereinigten Staaten. Unter ihnen befinden sich Breton, Ernst, Masson, Matta, Lam. Die Beispielhaftigkeit der surrealistischen Forschungen steck die Vereinigten Staaten förmlich an, während an Neo-Avantgarden des alten und neuen Kontinents übernehmen die Ideen der surrealistischen Meister, um neue Sprachen zu schaffen.	▮ La Seconde Guerre mondiale oblige de nombreux surréalistes à émigrer aux États-Unis : Breton, Ernst, Masson, Matta et Lam sont de ceux-là. L'exemple des recherches surréalistes se répand aux États-Unis. Quant aux nouvelles avant-gardes de l'Ancien comme du Nouveau Monde, elles vont partir des propositions des maîtres du surréalisme pour fonder de nouveaux langages.	▮ Door het uitbreken van de Tweede Wereldoorlog voelen veel surrealisten zich gedwongen naar de Verenigde Staten te emigreren. Enkele van hen zijn Breton, Ernst, Masson, Matta en Lam. De surrealistische kunstwerken zijn een voorbeeld voor kunstenaars in de Verenigde Staten. De nieuwe avant-garde van de Nieuwe Wereld en de Oude Wereld volgen de surrealistische meesters in het ontwikkelen van een nieuwe beeldtaal.

Glossary

Assemblage: generally applies to a three-dimensional collage, or a combination of objects and materials. It is similar to a collage, but defines itself as volume rather than as surface.

Automatic writing: also called "psychic automatism". A representational technique that consists in allowing the pen or brush to draw undirected, without control, without mental guidance imposed on the hand's movements. The subconscious expresses itself freely, so that images are summoned up from the depths without interference from the Super ego, in accordance with Freudian theory.

Cadavre exquis: french for "exquisite corpse". A group activity favoured by the Surrealists, its literal meaning refers to the paradoxical union of two random words in automatic writing. The group is seated around a table; one member begins to draw, then folds the paper and passes it to his neighbour, so that the drawing can be continued without knowledge of what had gone before. As in a game of consequences, the technique gives rise to strange monsters or incomprehensible images, the fruits of chance and of the psychological atmosphere cultivated by the group during the session. Use is made of the so-called method of "improbable association".

Collage: avant-garde experimental technique in which heterogeneous materials (newspaper cuttings, photos, objects, etc) are glued onto a surface that may have been variously prepared or painted. The materials may then undergo a pictorial intervention, being partially shaped or outlined.

Décollage: term invented by the surrealist writer Léo Malet, who in 1936 realised that the technique of collage would soon be transferred from small-scale collectors' pieces to much larger works in urban spaces, as indeed happened when avant-garde artists began to practise décollage.

Frottage: technique invented by the surrealist artist Max Ernst, borrowed from an infantile mode of expression. A soft pencil is rubbed on a piece of paper laid on a rough surface (a wooden floor, woven fabrics, leaves, bark, coins, etc) or one with variations of texture. The operation is mechanical, but the dynamism of the action is sufficient to activate the imagination, producing graphic results that are far more than the mere impression of an actual object. In the work of Ernst, in fact, the image develops through a complex process of alogical associations. The artist himself states that he takes part in the process "as a spectator".

Gouache: painting technique similar to water-colour, from which it differs by the addition of white chalk to lighten the colour of the pigments. Can be used on paper or on dry plaster.

Grattage: technique invented by the surrealist artist Max Ernst, borrowed like frottage from infantile behaviour. A wax crayon is rubbed on a piece of paper placed on a rough or textured surface.

Lithography: a method of printing. A design is drawn with a fatty or oily pencil on a limestone plate, and is then treated with acid which renders those areas not marked by the pencil repellent to ink. The ink thus adheres only to the design, which by the pressure of the press is transferred to paper.

Manifesto: a communicative strategy characteristic of avant-garde movements, which issue manifestos in order to proclaim their expressive choices, their ideology, their poetics. Such printed statements embody the principles, theories and programmes to which artists refer in creating a group or movement.

Object trouvé: french for "found object". It applies to an object found by an artist and generally selected – on account of its particular formal or stylistic features – so as to be elevated to the status of a work of art.

Oneiric activity: in psychoanalysis the term covers all the operations of sleep that transform various materials into visual narratives, i.e. dreams. Surrealism adopts the phrase as a guide to the production of works of art capable of elaborating and representing oneiric activity.

Papier collé: french for "pasted paper". Avant-garde experimental technique, in which pieces of paper of various provenance (such as fragments of newsprint or similar) are glued on to a surface that may have been prepared or painted. It differs from collage in that it makes use of no other material than paper.

Photomontage: technique for producing composite photographic images, obtained from different negatives so mounted as to form a single image that is visually plausible but frequently paradoxical. The simplest method is to assemble pieces of various photographs. More sophisticated effects can be obtained by retouching a photomontage, working directly on the negatives or on the photographic plate in the darkroom.

Rayograph: photogram technique devised by the Dadaist and surrealist Man Ray: the artist places objects directly onto photosensitive paper, without using any kind of camera, to create his transparent and kinetic images.

Ready-made: a neologism coined by Marcel Duchamp to indicate an existing object, used for artistic purposes and transformed into a work of art, one that is not made by him but merely indicated, pointed out. This operation was called "pointing" by Duchamp himself. The object is thereby subtracted from the everyday context, and loses its ordinary prerogatives to acquire new ones.

Rectified readymade: a readymade is said to be rectified when the artist makes some kind of intervention, adding or combining other objects.

Serigraphy: an ancient Chinese printing technique, adopted by avant-garde artists in the earlier twentieth century. A design is imposed on a screen of silk or other fine mesh, with blank areas coated with an impermeable substance, and ink is forced through the mesh onto the printing surface. It is a simple technique that allows for blocks of colour but no chiaroscuro.

Glossar

Assemblage: (aus dem französischen: Assemblage) wird normalerweise eine dreidimensionale Collage genannt. Genauer gesagt ist sie eine Kombination von Objekten und Materialien. Diese unterscheidet sich von der Collage, da sie als Volumen und nicht als Fläche dargestellt wird.

Automatisches Schreiben: auch "psychischer Automatismus" genannt. Eine Darstellungstechnik, die den Pinsel oder den Stift ohne einen Entwurf, ohne Kontrolle und eine überdachte Handbewegung malen lässt. Das Unterbewusstsein, den Theorien von Freud folgend, kann sich frei entfalten und lässt somit Bilder aus der Tiefe auftauchen, ohne Hemmungen des "Überichs".

Cadavre exquis: allgemeine Methode die von den Surrealisten benützt wird. Wörtlich übersetzt "ausgezeichneter Kadaver", eine Anspielung an die paradoxen Zusammenführung von zwei Wörtern, die zufällig den Anfang einer ersten Gemeinschaft des automatischen Schreibens entspricht. Die Gruppe setzte sich an einen Tisch und das erste Mitglied fing das Zeichnen an. Dann faltete dieser das Papier zusammen und überreichte es an den neben ihm sitzenden. Ohne das dieser sehen konnte was schon gezeichnet wurde musste er die Zeichnung weiter führen. Verglichen mit dem Flüsterpost-Spiel, entstehen durch diesen Vorgang komische Monster oder unverständliche Bilder. Diese ergaben sich durch Zufall und durch die mentale Atmosphäre, die während den Arbeitssitzungen der Gruppe herrschte. Somit wird die Methode der sogenannten "Zufallzusammensetzung" benützt.

Collage: (französischer Begriff) technik, von den künstlerischen Avantgarden experimentiert, in der man auf einer unterschiedlichst bearbeiteten und manchmal auch bemalten Fläche ungleiche Materialien (Schnipsel aus Zeitung, Foto, Objekte usw.) klebt. Diese können später auch bemalt oder mit Konturen betont werden.

Décollage: (französischer Begriff) begriff, der von dem Schriftsteller des späten Surrealismus Léo Malet erfunden wurde, der 1936 ansagt, dass die Collagetechnik vom kleinen Sammelwerk zum Großen, wie städtische Räume, übergehen würde. Dies geschah in den Experimenten der Neo-Avantgarden durch das Praktizieren der Decollage.

Fotomontage: prozedur, mit der man zusammengesetzte Fotobilder kreiert. Diese ergeben sich durch mehrere Negative, die zusammengeführt werden, um ein Bild zu formen, das optisch plausibel, aber meist paradox ist. Die einfachste Prozedur ist das Zusammensetzen von verschiedenen Fotografien. Raffiniertere Effekte erzeugt man durch die Bearbeitung oder durch die Fotobearbeitung einer Fotocollage in der man direkt das Negativ oder die Fotoplatte in der Dunkelkammer bearbeitet.

Frottage: eine Technik, die vom surrealistischen Künstler Max Ernst erfunden wurde und eine kindliche Ausdruckstechnik verwendet. Diese ergibt sich durch das Reiben eines weichen Bleistifts über ein Papier das auf einer Fläche liegt, die rau, faltig (Holzplatten eines Bodens, Relieftapeten, Folien, Baumrinden, Münzen usw.) oder mit leichten Vorsprüngen sein kann. Das Ausführen ist mechanisch, aber die Dynamik des Aktes ist ausreichend, um die Fantasie zu wecken und deswegen sieht man in den grafischen Drucken mehr als nur einen simplen Abdruck eines realen Objektes. So legt sich ein erfinderisches Vorgehen der Fantasie fest, das weit aus mehr ist als nur das automatische Übertragen eines realen Gegenstandes. Für Ernst ist nicht der Traum der Erzeuger eines Bildes, sondern das Gegenteil: das Bild ergibt sich durch ein komplexes Zusammenspiel von analogen Zusammenhängen. Der Künstler selbst wollte als "Zuschauer" dieser Prozedur mitwirken.

Gouache: oder Lache: Maltechnik ähnlich dem Aquarell, von dem sie sich durch das Beifügen von Deckweiß zum Aufhellen der Farben unterscheidet. Sie kann auf Papier oder trockenem Putz ausgeführt werden.

Grattage: eine Technik, die vom surrealistischen Künstler Max Ernst erfunden wurde und eine kindliche Ausdrucktechnik verwerdet, die das Gegenteil der Frottage ist. Diese ergibt sich durch das Reiben einer, mit Wachspastell, vorbereiteten Fläche über einer anderen, die faltig, rau oder mit leichten Vorsprüngen sein kann.

Lithografie: technische Prozedur, ähnlich dem Stich. Sie besteht aus dem Aufzeichnen eines

Bildes mit Kreidestiften auf Kalkstein. Dieser wird mit einer Säure behandelt, die mit der Farbe reagiert, die nicht vom Fett der Steinzeichnung geschützt ist. So haftet die Tinte nur auf dem aufgezeichnetem Bild, das durch eine Druckpresse auf Papier übertragen wird.

Manifest: charakteristische ommunikationstrategie der Avantgardebewegungen, die ihre Manifeste präsentieren, um ihre Wahl des Ausdrucks, idiologische Stellung und Poetik zu theoretisieren. In solchen Drucken werden so die Prinzipien, die Theorien und die Programme erklärt, auf welche sie sich für die Gründung von einer Gruppe oder Bewegung beziehen.

Objet trouvée: (französischer Ausdruck, wörtlich übersetzbar mit "gefundener Gegenstand"). Steht für einen Gegenstand, der vom Künstler gefunden wurde und meist wegen dessen außergewöhnlichen Form oder Stils ausgewählt wird, wodurch es zu einem Kunstwerk wird.

Papier collé (Geklebtes Papier): (französischer Ausdruck) Technik, von den künstlerischen Avantgarden experimentiert, in der man auf einer unterschiedlichst bearbeiteten und manchmal auch bemalten Fläche ausschließlich Papiermaterialien von ungleicher Herkunft (Zeitungsausschnitte oder von andere Papierarten) klebt. Somit unterscheidet sich diese von der Collage, da nur Papier benutzt wird und keine anderen Materialien.

Rayographie: genaugenommen "Graphie von Ray". Eine Technik, die ursprünglich vom Dada und dem surrealistischen Künstler Man Ray entwickelt wurde: Der Künstler legt die Gegenstände direkt auf das emulgierte lichtempfindliche Papier, ohne einen Fotoapparat zu nutzen und verwendet neue Materialien für seine durchsichtigen und kinetischen Skulpturen.

Ready-made (fertig gestellt): (englischer Begriff, wörtlich "schon gemacht" - "fertig gestellt"). Neologismus von Marcel Duchamp geprägt, um einen schon fertig gestellten Gegenstand zu bezeichnen, welches dann vom Künstler auf künstlerischer Art benützt wird und als Kunstwerk zu betrachten ist. Obwohl dieser vom Künstler gemacht wurde, wird ihm es nur zugeschrieben und angezeigt. Dieser Vorgang wird von Duchamp persönlich als "Pointing" benannt. Der Gegenstand ist also aus dem Alltag genommen und verliert sein ursprünglichen Zweck, um einen anderen zu bekommen.

Serigrafie: eine Drucktechnik aus der chinesischen Antike, die von den Avantgarde-Künstlern zu Beginn des 20.Jhdts übernommen wird. Eine Grundform wird ohne Druck auf eine Oberfläche übertragen: durch ein Seidentuch, welches mit Kleber oder geeigneten Schablonen an den gewünschten Stellen abgedichtet wurde, wird die Tinte mit Hilfe einer Gummischaufel direkt auf ein darunter liegendes Blatt Papier filtriert. Dem Bild folgend wird die Tinte nur durch die unbedeckten Stellen fließen. Eine einfache Technik, die es ermöglicht, platte und nicht helldunkle Farben zu erzielen.

Traumdarstellung: in der Psychoanalyse beinhaltet dieser Begriff alle Traumvorgänge, da alle Materialien zu sichtbaren Geschichten umgewandelt werden. Der Surrealismus lehnt sich an diesen Begriff an und nützt ihn als Führer für die Herstellung von Kunstwerken, welche in der Lage sind eine Traumarbeit zu entwerfen und darzustellen.

Verbessertes Ready-made : ein Ready-made wird als „Verbessert" bezeichnet, wenn der Künstler es bearbeitet, mit anderen Gegenständen kombiniert, oder neue hinzufügt.

Glossaire

Assemblage : désigne généralement un collage à trois dimensions, ou une combinaison d'objets et de matériaux. Apparenté au collage, l'assemblage s'en distingue en se présentant comme volume et non comme superficie.

« Cadavre Exquis » : pratique collective affectionnée par les surréalistes. Il s'agit de faire composer une phrase ou un dessin par plusieurs personnes sans qu'aucune puisse voir ce qui a été écrit ou dessiné précédemment. L'expérience est proche de l'écriture automatique. Le groupe se disposait autour d'une table : un des membres commençait un dessin sur un papier qu'il pliait ensuite avant de le passer à son voisin pour qu'il « continuât » le dessin sans savoir ce qui avait été dessiné au préalable, et ainsi de suite. Ce genre d'opération fait naître d'étranges monstres ou des images incompréhensibles, résultats du hasard, des profondeurs de l'inconscient et de l'ambiance psychologique générale dans laquelle le groupe avait préalablement travaillé. Ce processus utilise donc le procédé des « associations improbables ».

Collage : technique expérimentée par les avant-gardes artistiques, dans laquelle on « colle » sur une surface préparée, éventuellement colorée, des matériaux hétéroclites et hétérogènes (coupures de journal, photographies, objets etc.). Ces matériaux peuvent ensuite subir une intervention picturale ou des manipulations diverses.

Décollage : définition inventée par Léo Malet en 1936 : cet écrivain surréaliste tardif anticipe alors que le processus du collage serait bientôt transféré de l'échelle réduite de l'œuvre de collection à celle – plus vaste – des espaces urbains. Ce que les expérimentations des nouvelles avant-gardes allaient effectivement réaliser.

Écriture automatique : également qualifiée d'« automatisme psychique », cette technique de représentation – transposée du travail littéraire et inventée par Breton – consiste à laisser le pinceau ou la plume errer sur le support choisi sans projet ni contrôle, sans aucune directive mentale imposée au mouvement de la main. L'inconscient est alors censé s'exprimer en toute liberté, laissant apparaître les images issues des profondeurs de l'être, sans les inhibitions dues au « surmoi » tel qu'il est décrit par Freud.

Frottage : technique inventée par l'artiste surréaliste Max Ernst et reprenant un mode d'expression enfantin. Elle consiste à frotter un crayon gras sur une feuille préalablement posée sur une surface rugueuse ou inégale (lame de parquet, tapisserie en relief, feuille, pierre, écorce d'arbre, pièce de monnaie etc.). L'opération est mécanique, mais la dynamique même de l'action exercée est suffisante pour stimuler l'imagination, qui verra dans l'empreinte graphique obtenue bien autre chose que le simple « calque » d'un objet réel. On détermine ainsi un processus créatif qui va au-delà de la pure transcription automatique d'un objet. Chez Ernst, ce n'est pas le rêve qui crée alors l'objet, mais l'inverse : l'image se développe à travers un jeu complexe d'associations alogiques. Le même artiste affirmait assister ainsi « en spectateur » au processus de création.

Gouache : technique picturale proche de l'aquarelle – dont elle diffère toutefois par l'adjonction de blanc de céruse pour éclaircir les couleurs. On peut l'exécuter sur papier, mais aussi sur enduit sec.

Grattage : technique inventée par l'artiste surréaliste Max Ernst, en reprenant un mode d'expression enfantin proche du frottage (voir ce mot). On la met en œuvre en grattant un support préalablement préparé au pastel cireux et posé sur une surface rugueuse ou inégale.

Lithographie : procédé technique proche de la gravure. Il consiste à tracer un dessin avec une mine grasse sur une surface de pierre calcaire (dite « pierre lithographique »). Celle-ci est ensuite traitée avec un acide qui interdit l'encrage ailleurs que sur le tracé au crayon gras. Il suffira ensuite d'imprimer sur une feuille le dessin ainsi encré.

Manifeste : technique de communication caractéristique des mouvements d'avant-garde qui présentent par ce moyen leurs positions idéologiques, leur poétique, leurs choix expressifs, etc. Seront ainsi imprimés les principes et les programmes auxquels les artistes font référence lors de la création d'un groupe ou d'un mouvement.

Objet trouvé : il s'agit d'un objet repéré par hasard, puis choisi par l'artiste pour ses caractéristiques formelles ou stylistiques, et élevé par cet artiste au rang d'œuvre d'art.

Papiers collés : technique mise en œuvre par les avant-gardes artistiques, consistant à « coller » sur une surface préparée, éventuellement colorée, des matériaux hétérogènes, mais exclusivement à support de papier (coupures de journaux, cartons découpés, etc). Cette technique diffère du collage (voir ce mot) par le refus de tout matériau autre que le papier.

Photomontage : procédé qui permet d'obtenir des images photographiques composites à partir de divers négatifs montés ensemble, de façon à former des représentations visuellement plausibles mais souvent paradoxales. Le mode opératoire le plus simple consiste à assembler sur un même support des fragments de diverses photographies. On obtient des effets plus raffinés en retouchant des clichés par intervention directe sur le négatif ou sur la plaque photographique, en chambre noire.

Rayographie : technique de « représentation » mise au point par l'artiste dada et surréaliste Man Ray. L'artiste pose un objet directement sur le papier photosensible, sans utiliser d'appareil photographique ; la manipulation permet d'obtenir de véritables images cinétiques.

Ready-made : (expression anglaise signifiant « tout fait », « prêt à l'emploi ».) Néologisme inventé par Marcel Duchamp pour désigner un objet déjà fabriqué et couramment disponible, mais sélectionné par l'artiste pour l'élever au rang d'œuvre d'art. Cette opération est appelée *pointing* par son inventeur. Prélevé dans le quotidien, l'objet perd alors ses prérogatives usuelles pour en acquérir d'autres.

Ready-made rectifié : un *ready-made* est ainsi qualifié lorsque l'artiste intervient sur l'objet choisi ou y ajoute d'autres éléments.

Sérigraphie : technique d'impression ancienne, d'origine chinoise, reprise et adoptée par diverses avant-gardes artistiques du xxe siècle. À travers un écran de soie tendu sur une feuille de papier et rendu imperméable à des endroits prédéterminés, au moyen de colle ou de caches appropriés, on fait filtrer de l'encre colorée au moyen d'une palette en caoutchouc. Suivant le dessin, la couleur ne se déposera ainsi que sur les parties découvertes. Cette technique simple permet d'obtenir des couleurs en à-plat, sans modelé de clair-obscur.

Travail onirique : en psychanalyse, cette expression définit et regroupe toutes les opérations du rêve, lorsqu'il transforme ses divers éléments en récits visuels. Le surréalisme intègre et justifie cette opération comme guide de production pour des travaux artistiques, capables d'élaborer et de représenter le rêve.

Verklarende Woordenlijst

Assemblage: algemene term voor een driedimensionale collage of een combinatie van voorwerpen en materialen. Verwant aan de collage met het verschil dat het niet oppervlakkig is, maar volume heeft.

Automatisch schrift: ook wel "psychisch automatisme" genoemd. Beeldtechniek waarbij men de pen of tekenpen zonder vooropgezet plan over het papier laat gaan, zonder controle en zonder een mentale sturing van de handbeweging. Het onderbewuste, dat spontaan wordt ontsloten zonder remmingen van het superego en onder invloed van Freudiaanse theorieën, produceert beelden die uit het binnenste komen.

Cadavre exquis: collectieve activiteit die door de surrealisten werd gepraktiseerd. Letterlijk 'uitmuntend lijk'. Een toespeling op de paradoxale vereniging van twee toevallige beginwoorden die voortkomen uit het automatisch schrijven (*écriture automatique*). De groep zit rond een tafel. Iemand begint te tekenen, draait dan het papier om en geeft het door aan degene die naast hem zit. Deze gaat verder met de tekening zonder te weten wat er in een eerder stadium is getekend. Vergelijkbaar met het spel van de telegraaf zonder draden. In dit spel verschijnen vreemde monsters of onbegrijpelijke beelden als gevolg van de algemene psychologische atmosfeer die er tijdens de seance heerste. Men maakte dus gebruik van de methode van de 'onwaarschijnlijke associaties'.

Collage: experimentele techniek van de avant-garde. Op een oppervlak worden verschillend geprepareerde en eventueel met pigmenten gekleurde heterogene materialen gelijmd (krantenknipsels, foto's, voorwerpen enz.). Deze materialen kunnen vervolgens weer worden beschilderd, gemodelleerd of omlijnd.

Decollage: uitgevonden door de laat surrealistische schrijver Léo Malet. Hij voorziet in 1936 dat de collage als klein verzamelwerk op veel grotere schaal in de stedelijke ruimte zal verschijnen. Dit gebeurde inderdaad tijdens de decollage-experimenten van de neo-avantgarde.

Droomarbeid: in de psychoanalyse verstaat men onder droomarbeid alle werkzame processen tijdens het dromen, waarin het verschillende materiaal wordt omgevormd tot visuele voorstellingen. Het surrealisme neemt deze term over als leidraad voor kunst die droomarbeid kan uitwerken en verbeelden.

Fotomontage: methode waarmee samengestelde fotobeelden worden verkregen. Verschillende negatieven worden samengevoegd en vormen een ogenschijnlijk plausibel, maar vaak paradoxaal beeld. De meest eenvoudige procedure bestaat uit het assembleren van verschillende foto's. Meer geraffineerde effecten worden bereikt door het negatief of de filmstrook in de donkere kamer bij te werken of te retoucheren.

Frottage: techniek uitgevonden door de surrealist Max Ernst, waarin gebruik wordt gemaakt van een kinderlijke expressievorm. Met een zacht potlood wordt over een vel papier gewreven dat op een ruw oppervlak ligt (gelinieerd vloeroppervlak, stoffering in reliëf, bladeren, boomschors, munten enz.) of op een oppervlak met lichte verdikkingen. Het is een mechanische handeling, waarvan de dynamische actie voldoende is om de verbeelding te activeren. Men ziet hierdoor meer in de grafische voorstelling dan een simpele afdruk van een bestaand voorwerp. Op deze manier wordt een verbeeldingsproces vastgelegd dat verder gaat dan alleen de automatische transcriptie van een bestaand voorwerp. Bij Max Ernst creëert niet de droom het beeld, integendeel: het beeld ontstaat door een complex spel van onlogische associaties. De kunstenaar zegt in feite dat hij 'als toeschouwer' aan dit proces deelneemt.

Gewijzigde Ready made: een ready-made is gewijzigd als de kunstenaar een ingreep heeft gedaan of andere voorwerpen toevoegt of combineert.

Gouache: een schildertechniek, verwant aan de aquarel, waarin loodwit wordt gebruikt om de kleuren lichter te maken. Gouache kan op papier, maar ook op droog pleisterkalk worden gebruikt.

Grattage: techniek die door de surrealist Max Ernst is uitgevonden, waarbij een kinderlijke expressievorm wordt toegepast die verwant is aan de frottage. Een oppervlak dat met waskrijt is geprepareerd, wordt afgeschraapt en op een ruw oppervlak of op een ondergrond van ongelijke dikte gelegd. Het is een mechanische handeling, waarvan de dynamische actie voldoende is om de verbeelding te activeren. De grafische voorstelling maakt veel meer zichtbaar dan alleen de simpele afdruk van een bestaand voorwerp.

Lithografie: technisch werkwijze verwant aan de gravure. Op een kalksteenplaat wordt met vet krijt een tekening gemaakt. Deze wordt vervolgens behandeld met een zuur dat de gedeelten die niet door het vet van de tekening zijn beschermd, water- en inktafstotend maakt. De inkt hecht alleen op de tekening. Het vel papier wordt vervolgens onder een drukpers doorgehaald.

Manifest: communicatiestrategie, kenmerkend voor avant-gardestromingen. Door middel van manifesten theoretiseert de avant-garde haar artistieke keuzes, ideologische posities en poëtica. In deze gedrukte manifesten werden dus principes, theorieën en programma's verklaard, waaraan de kunstenaars in de kunstuiting van een groep of stroming refereerden.

Objet trouvé: (Fr. letterlijk vertaald 'gevonden voorwerp'). Een voorwerp dat door de kunstenaar is gevonden en meestal is uitgekozen vanwege karakteristieke formele of stilistische kenmerken en vervolgens tot kunstwerk wordt verheven.

Papier collé: experimentele techniek van de avant-garde. Op een oppervlak worden verschillende geprepareerde en eventueel met pigmenten gekleurde papieren van heterogene afkomst gelijmd(krantenknipsels of andere stukken papier). Het verschilt van de collage doordat er alleen papier en geen andere materialen wordt gebruikt.

Rayografie: rayografen van Man Ray (pseudoniem). Een techniek die voor het eerst werd toegepast door dadaïst en surrealist Man Ray: de kunstenaar plaatst voorwerpen direct op het lichtgevoelige materiaal, zonder tussenkomst van het fototoestel en gebruikt nieuwe materialen voor zijn transparante en kinetische beelden.

Ready-made: (Eng. letterlijk 'klaar voor gebruik', 'pasklaar'). Een neologisme bedacht door Marcel Duchamp om een bestaand voorwerp mee aan te duiden dat een kunstwerk wordt door het simpele feit dat de kunstenaar het heeft aangewezen en uitgezocht. Deze handeling werd door Duchamp zelf *pointing* genoemd. Het voorwerp is uit zijn context gehaald. Het verliest daardoor zijn oorspronkelijke eigenschappen en gebruik en krijgt andere eigenschappen.

Zeefdruk: oude Chinese druktechniek die doorde avant-gardebe-wegingen in de eerste en tweede helft van de twintigste eeuw is overgenomen. Voorafgaand aan de overgang van de matrijs naar het afdrukken zonder drukkracht. Door een stuk zijde, waarvan delen die met lijm of afdeklak zijn vastgezet waterafstotend blijven, wordt de inkt met behulp van een rakel direct op het onderliggende blad papier gefilterd. De kleur dringt alleen door in de onbedekte delen van het ontwerp. Het is een eenvoudige techniek waarmee alleen vlakke kleurvlakken en geen licht-donker effecten worden verkregen.

Biographies
Biografien
Biografieën

Jean (Hans) Arp
Strasbourg 1887 - Basel 1966

1911	Studied in Weimar and Berlin / Studien in Weimar und Berlin / Études à Weimar et à Berlin / Studeert in Weimar en in Berlijn
1912-1914	*Terrestrial form* / *Irdische Formen* / *Formes terrestres* / *Aardse Vormen* (Museum of Modern Art, New York)
1914	Travelled to Paris to escape the war. Left France after being arrested / Nach Paris, um dem Krieg zu entgehen; er wird verhaftet und muss Frankreich verlassen / Vient à Paris pour éviter la guerre / Gaat naar Parijs om de oorlog te vermijden. Wordt gearresteerd, moet Frankrijk verlaten
1919	Köln: Founded the Dada group with Max Ernst / Mit Max Ernst gründet er die Dada Gruppe / Fonde le groupe *Dada* avec Max Frnst / Richt met Max Ernst de groep Dada op
1921	Paris: Worked with Tristan Tzara and Max Ernst. Surrealist experimentation / Arbeitet er mit Tristan Tzara und Max Ernst. Surrealistische Recherchen / Travaille avec Tristan Tzara et Max Ernst. Fait des recherches sur le surréalisme / Werkt samen met Tristan Tzara en Max Ernst. Surrealistische experimenten
1925	Paris: Took part in first surrealist exhibition / Nimmt er an der Ersten Ausstellung der surrealistischen Gruppe teil / Participe à la première exposition du groupe surréaliste / Neemt deel aan de eerste tentoonstelling van de surrealisten
1930-1931	Joined avant-garde groups *Cercle et Carré* and *Abstraction-Création* / Er schließt sich den avantgardistischen Gruppen *Cercle et Carré* und *Abstraction-Création* an / Adhère au groupe d'avant-garde *Cercle et Carré* et *Abstraction-Création* / Sluit zich aan bij de avantgardistische groepen *Cercle et Carré* en *Abstraction-Création*
1940-1960	Associated with the marble workers in Carrara and Pietrasanta / Er frequentiert di Marmor Werkstätten in Carrara und Pietrasanta / Fréquente les laboratoires des marbres de Carrare et de Pietrasanta / Bezoekt vaak de marmerwerkplaatsen van Carrara en Pietrasanta

Hans Bellmer
Kattowitz 1902 - Paris 1975

1922-1924	Berlin
	Contact with Otto Dix and George Grosz. Started painting and illustration / Treffen mit Otto Dix und George Grosz. Annäherung an die Malerei und die Illustration / Rencontre avec Otto Dix et Georg Grosz. Aborde la peinture et l'illustration / Ontmoet Otto Dix en George Grosz. Wijdt zich aan schilderkunst en illustraties
1930-1933	Paris: Contact with the Surrealists / Schließt er sich der Gruppe der Surrealisten an / Entre dans le groupe surréaliste / Sluit zich aan bij de surrealisten
	Die Puppe, Bellmer's book with a series of photographs of his doll project / *Die Puppe*: Fotoserie einer ausgekugelten Puppe / Réalise les séries suivantes de *Die Puppe* / Verwezenlijkt *Die Puppe*, serie van foto's van een ontwrichte pop
1934	Surrealist journal *Minotaure* published series of photographs of his dismembered doll / Die Zeitschrift *Minotaure* veröffentlicht Fotos der ersten Serie von *Die Puppe* / La revue *Le Minotaure* publie la première série de *Die Puppe* (*La Poupée*), photos d'une poupée désarticulée / Het tijdschrift *Minotaure* pubbliceert de foto's van de eerste serie van *Die Puppe*
1935-1940	His photographs illustrated books by Hoffmann and Éluard / Er illustriert Bücher von Hoffmann und Éluard mit seinen Fotos / Illustre les livres de Hoffmann et de Paul Éluard avec ses photos / Illustreert boeken van Hoffmann en Éluard met zijn foto's
1968	*Petit Traité de morale* published with a series of engravings / Publikation mit raffinierten Radierungen / Publication illustrée de dessins raffinés / Publicatie met verfijnde ontwerpen

André Breton
Tinchebray 1896 - Paris 1966
1900-1907 Studied in Paris. Writer and poet with a passion for art / Studien in Paris; als Schriftsteller und Poet begeistert er sich für die Kunst / Études à Paris. Écrivain et poète, se passionne pour l'art / Studeert in Parijs. Is schrijver en dichter en ontwikkelt een passie voor kunst
1913 Enrolled in Faculty of Medicine but continued to write poetry / Er schreibt sich an der medizinischen Fakultät ein und fährt fort, Verse zu schreiben / S'inscrit à la faculté de médecine et continue à composer des vers / Schrijft zich in bij de Faculteit Medicijnen en blijft gedichten schrijven
1915 Enlisted, served in neuro-psychiatric centre / Er wird in den Krieg eingezogen und leistet in einem Zentrum für Neuropsychiatrie seinen Kriegsdienst / Mobilisé pendant la guerre, est enrôlé dans un centre neuropsychiatrique / Gerekruteerd voor de oorlog, verleent dienst in een neuro-psychiatrische inrichting
1917 Contributed to *Mercure de France* and made contact with Dada circle / Er schreibt für den *Mercure de France* und nimmt Kontakt mit der Dada Szene auf / Écrit dans *Le Mercure de France* et entre en contact avec le milieu dada / Schrijft voor *Mercure de France*, komt in aanraking met de Dada wereld
1921 Wien: Visited Sigmund Freud / Besuch bei Sigmund Freud / Rend visite à Sigmund Freud / Bezoekt Sigmund Freud
1924 *First Surrealist manifesto* / *Erstes Manifest des Surrealismus* / *Premier manifeste du surréalisme* / *Eerste Surrealistisch Manifest*
1929 *Second Surrealist manifesto* / *Zweites Manifest des Surrealismus* / *Second manifeste du surréalisme* / *Tweede Surrealistisch Manifest*
1937 Published *L'amour fou* / Publie *L'Amour fou* / Er publiziert *L'amour fou* / Publiceert *L'amour fou*

Joseph Cornell
Nyack, New York 1903 - New York 1972
1931 New York, Levy Gallery: Visited the Surrealist exhibition and identified with their poetry / Er sieht die Ausstellung der Surrealisten und nähert sich ihrer Poetik / Voit l'exposition des surréalistes et se rapproche de leur théorie poétique / Bezichtigt de tentoonstelling van de surrealisten en sluit zich aan bij hun dichtkunst
1932 New York, Levy Gallery: First one-man show. Exhibited his first *Shadow Boxes* / Erste Einzelausstellung mit den ersten *Shadow Boxes* / Première exposition personnelle. Expose ses premières *Shadow Boxes* (Boîtes à ombres) / Eerste persoonlijke tentoonstelling. Exposeert de eerste *Shadow Boxes*
1936 *Untitled Soap Bubble Set* (Wadsworth Atheneum, Hartford, Connecticut): first exhibition of a new series of boxes containing objects / Erstes Beispiel einer neuen Serie von Schachteln, die Gegenstände beinhalten / Premier exemple d'une nouvelle série de boîtes contenant des objets / Eerste voorbeeld van een nieuwe serie doosjes met voorwerpen erin
1950 Two dimensional Collage of magazine cuttings / Zweidimensionale Collage mit Zeitschriftenausschnitten / Collages bidimensionnels avec des journaux découpés / Tweedimensionale collage met tijdschriftknipsels
1950-1970 Boxes influential in development of Pop culture / Starker Einfluss seiner Schachteln auf die Pop Bewegung / Grande influence de ses boîtes dans la recherche pop / Grote invloed van zijn doosjes op de popwereld

Salvador Dalí
Figueres 1904 -1989
1922-1925 Madrid: Friendship with Luis Buñuel and Federico Garcia Lorca / Freundschaft mit Luis Buñuel und Federico García Lorca / Se lie d'amitié avec Luis Buñuel et Federico Garcia Lorca / Raakt bevriend met Luis Buñuel en Federico Garcia Lorca
1925 Exhibited in Barcellona / Ausstellung in Barcelona / Expose à Barcelone / Exposeert in Barcelona
1926 Paris: Met Picasso / Begegnet er Picasso / Rencontre Picasso / Ontmoet Picasso
1929 Paris: presented the film *Le chien andalou* at the Studio 28 with Buñuel / Präsentiert er im Studio 28 mit Buñuel den Film *Le chien andalou* / Avec Buñuel, présente le film *Le Chien andalou* au Studio 28 / Vertoont met Buñuel de film *Un chien andalou* in Studio 28
1930 Bought a cabin at Port Lligat, near Cadaqués / Umzug nach Cadaqués, in die Ortschaft Port Lligat, wo er ein Haus kauft / S'installe à Cadaquès, dans la localité de Port Lligat, où il achète une maison / Verhuist naar Cadaqués, in de buurt van Port Lligat, waar hij een huis koopt
1933 Paris, Galerie Pierre Colle: Third one-man show: included the *Retrospective bust of a woman* / Dritte Einzelausstellung: er präsentiert Objekte und die *Retrospektive Frauenbüste* / Troisième exposition personnelle : il présente *Buste rétrospectif de femme* / Derde persoonlijke tentoonstelling: waar *de Retrospectieve Vrouwenbuste*, en andere objecten tentoon worden gesteld (Museum of Modern Art, New York)
1936 Exhibited in Paris, London, New York; immortalised on the cover of *Time* magazine / Ausstellungen in Paris, London und New York; Er wird auf dem Titelblatt des *Time* abgebildet / Expose à Paris, Londres, New York; fait la une de *Time* : le voilà immortalisé / Exposeert in Parijs, Londen en New York; Wordt onsterfelijk door de cover van de *Time*
1938 London: Visited Sigmund Freud and showed him *Metamorphosis of Narcissus* / Besucht er Sigmund Freud und zeigt ihm das Gemälde *Die Metamorphose des Narziss* / Rend visite à Sigmund Freud et lui montre le tableau *Métamorphoses de Narcisse* / Bezoekt Sigmund Freud en toont hem het schilderij *Metamorfose van Narcissus* (Tate Gallery, London)
1939-1947 In United States during war / Während der Kriegsjahre lebt er in den Vereinigten Staaten / Vit aux États-Unis durant les années de guerre / Woont in de Verenigde Staten gedurende de oorlogsjaren

---

Giorgio De Chirico
Vólos 1888 - Roma 1978
1895-1905 Childhood in Vólos / Kindheit in Vólos / Enfance à Vólos / Jeugd in Vólos
1905 Münich
1909 Florence: first experience of the metaphysical / Erste metaphysische Erfahrungen / Premières expériences métaphysiques / Eerste metafysische ervaringen
1911 Paris
L'enigma dell'ora / *Das Rätsel der Stunde* / *L'Énigme de l'heure* / *Das Rätsel der Stunde* (Private Collection, Milano); *Piazze d'Italia* series / *Italienischen Plätze* / Places d'Italie / Pleinen van Italië
1912 Exhibited in Paris. Praised by Apollinaire / Er stellt in Paris aus und wird von Apollinaire geschätzt / Expose à Paris. Apprécié par Apollinaire / Exposeert in Parijs en wordt gewaardeerd door Apollinaire
1917 Ferrara: Met Carlo Carrà / trifft er Carlo Carrà / Rencontre Carlo Carrà / Ontmoet Carlo Carrà
Began Metaphysical movement / Es beginnt die metaphysische Bewegung / Lance le mouvement de la peinture « métaphysique » / Start de beweging van de Metafysica
Hector and Andromache / *Hektor und Andromache* / *Hector et Andromaque, Hektor en Andromache* (Private Collection, Milano
Maniquin paintings / Phase der Bilder mit den Gelenkpuppen / Période des tableaux avec mannequins / Periode van schilderijen met etalagepoppen

1919   Rome: Joined *Valori Plastici* movement and contributed to the journal of same name Wrote *Ebdomero* / Er schließt sich der Bewegung und Zeitschrift *Valori Plastici* an Er schreibt *Ebdomero* / Adhère au mouvement et à la revue des *Valeurs plastiques* Écrit *Hebdomeros* / Sluit zich aan bij de beweging en het tijdschrift Valori Plastici, Schrijft *Hebdomeros*

1924-1934   Paris: Frequented surrealist circle: his contribution is recognised / Er schließt sich den Surrealisten an, wobei er als Inspirator der Bewegung gilt / Entre dans le milieu surréaliste où il est reconnu comme inspirateur du mouvement / Betreedt de wereld van de surrealisten, waar hij wordt erkend als inspiratiebron van de beweging

1945-1955   Roma: Continued to paint / Er malt weiter / Continue à peindre / Blijft doorgaan met schilderen

---

Paul Delvaux
Antheit 1897 - Furnes 1994

1920-1924   Brussel: Studied painting and architecture at the Academy of Fine Arts / Studiert er Malerei und Architektur an der Akademie der Schönen Künste / Étudie la peinture et l'architecture à l'Académie des beaux-arts / Studeert schilderkunst en architectuur aan de Academie voor Schone Kunsten

1925   Brussel: First one-man show / Erste Einzelausstellung / Première exposition personnelle / Eerste persoonlijke tentoonstelling

1925-1935   Surrealist painting influenced by De Chirico and Magritte / Surrealistischer Stil, beeinflusst durch die Malerei von De Chirico und Magritte / Style surréaliste, influencé par la peinture de De Chirico et Magritte / Surrealistische stijl, beïnvloedt door de schilderijen van De Chirico en Magritte

1937   *L'Aurore* (Collezione Peggy Guggenheim, Venezia)

1940-1950   Murals in the Palais des Congrès Brussels, in the Casinò in Ostende and in the Institute of Zoology in Liège / Ausführung von Wandmalereien am Kongresspalast Brüssel, im Casino von Ostende und am Zoologischen Institut Lüttich / Effectue les peintures murales au Palais des Congrès de Brussel et à l'Institut de zoologie de Liège / Verwezenlijkt de muurschilderingen in het Congresgebouw van Brussel, het Casino van Oostende en het Zoölogisch Instituut van Luik

---

Marcel Duchamp
Blainville 1887 - Neuilly-sur-Seine 1968

1904   Paris: Influence of Cézanne-Cubists / Studiert er Cézanne und den Kubismus / Recherches sur Cézanne et le cubisme / Experimenteert met het cézanniaans-Kubisme

1913   New York: Exhibited at Armory Show: *Nude descending a staircase* / Armory Show: er stellt den *Akt, Eine Treppe hinuntersteigend* aus / Exposition à l'Armory Show. Expose *Nu descendant un escalier* / Tentoonstelling in de Armory Show: stelt *Naakt de trap aflopend tentoon* (Philadelphia Museum of Art, Philadelphia)
The Large Glass / *Das Große Glas* / *Grote Glasraam* (Philadelphia Museum of Art, Philadelphia)
First *Readymades* / Die ersten *Readymades* / Commence les premiers *ready-mades* / Begint aan de eerste *ready mades*

1918   Buenos Aires: Spent following years playing chess / Er widmet sich ausschließlich dem Schachspiel / Se consacre exclusivement au jeu d'échecs / Legt zich uitsluitend toe op hets chaakspel

1919   Paris: Encounter with Surrealists / Begegnet er den Surrealisten / Il rencontre les surréalistes / Keert terug naar Parijs, ontmoet de surrealisten
Readymades L.H.O.O.Q (Private Collection / Privatsammlung / Collection privée / Privécollectie;

50 cc de Paris (Philadelphia Museum of Art, Philadelphia)

1920-1923 First kinetic works / Konstruktion der ersten optisch-kinetischen Reliefs / Construit les premiers reliefs optico-cinétiques / Vervaardigt de eerste optische-kinetische reliëfs

1923 Stopped work on *The Large Glass* / *Das Große Glas* bleibt definitiv unvollendet / *Le Grand verre* est laissé inachevé définitivement / Het *Grote Glasraam* blijft definitief onvoltooid

1925-1926 In collaboration with Man Ray filmed the Rotoreliefs as *Anémic Cinéma* / Mit Man Ray dreht er den Kurzfilm *Anémic Cinéma* / Réalise avec Man Ray un petit film, *Anemic Cinema* / Verwezenlijkt met Man Ray de korte film *Anémic Cinéma*

1969 Philadelphia Museum of Art: Exhibited posthumous *Étant donnés* tableau / Wir nach seinem Tod sein Werk *Étant donnés* vorgestellt / Présentation de l'œuvre posthume *Étant donnés* / Het postuum werk *Étant donnés* wordt getoond

Max Ernst
Brühl 1891 - Paris 1976

1913 Berlin: Emerged as a painter in the Expressionist group / Debütiert er als Maler mit den Expressionisten / Débute comme peintre avec le groupe expressionniste / Debuteert als schilder met de expressionisten

1914 Köln: Met Hans Arp / Trifft er auf Hans Arp / Rencontre Hans Arp / Ontmoet Hans arp

1919 München: Visited Paul Klee at his studio / Besuch im Atelier von Paul Klee / Visite l'atelier de Paul Klee / Bezoekt het atelier van Paul Klee

Met Hugo Ball and the Dada group in Zurich / Er lernt Hugo Ball und den Züricher Dadaismus kennen / Fait la connaissance d'Hugo Ball et des activités du mouvement dada zurichois / Leert Hugo Ball en zijn bezigheden als Zürichse Dadaïst kennen

Köln: Founded a Dada group with Arp and Baargeld / En gründet mit Arp und Baargeld eine Dada Gruppe / Avec Arp et Baargeld, fonde un groupe / Richt een Dada-groep op, samen met arp en Baargeld

1922 Left Cologne to join the Éluard couple in Paris / Er verlässt Köln und folgt dem Ehepaar Éluard nach Paris / Quitte Cologne et rejoint le couple Éluard à Paris / Verlaat Keulen en gaat naar het echtpaar Éluard in Parijs

Les Malheurs des Immortels, rélévés par Paul Éluard et Max Ernst, twenty texts by Éluard illustrated withcollage drawings by Ernst / Es wird *Les Malheurs des Immortels, rélévés par Paul Éluard et Max Ernst* veröffentlicht, eine Sammlung von zwanzig Texten von Éluard, illustriert mit Collage-Zeichnungen von Ernst / Publication des *Malheurs des Immortels, relevés par Paul Eluard et Max Ernst*, un recueil de vingt textes d'Eluard illustrés par ses dessins collages / *Les Malheurs des Immortels, rélévés par Paul Éluard et Max Ernst*, een verzameling van twintig teksten van Éluard, geïllustreerd met een tekeningencollage van Ernst, wordt gepubliceerd

1925 Invented the frottage technique, using rubbings as a source of images / Er erfindet die Frottage Technik für die Herstellung automatischer Bilder / Invente la technique du frottage pour réaliser des images automatiques / Vindt de frottage-techniek uit voor de verwezenlijking van automatische afbeeldingen

1935-1936 Developed the decalcomania technique / Entwicklung der Dekalkomanie Technik / Développe la technique de la décalcomanie / Ontwikkelt de decalcotechniek

1954 Venezia: Won the Gran Premio for painting at the Biennale / Großer Preis für Malerei auf der Biennale / Remporte le grand prix de peinture à la Biennale / Wint de Grote Prijs voor de schilderkunst tijdens de Biënnale

Alberto Giacometti
Borgonovo di Stampa 1901 - Chur 1966
1925-1931 Studied in Paris / Studien in Paris / Études à Paris / Studeert in Parijs
Influenced by Brancusi, Laurens, Lipchitz / Beeinflussung durch Brancusi, Laurens und Lipchitz / Subit l'influence de Brancusi, Laurens, Lipchitz /Ondergaat de invloed van Brâncuşi, Laurens en Lipchitz
Interest in primitive art and attracted to surrealist groups / Es reift sein Interesse für die primitive Kunst und er nähert sich den surrealistischen Gruppen / S'intéresse de plus en plus à l'art primitif et se rapproche des groupes surréalistes / Vergroot de interesse voor de primitieve kunst en sluit zich aan bij de surrealisten
1948 New York, Pierre Matisse Gallery: Exhibited first mature works: extremely elongated bodies / Stellt er die ersten Werke seiner stilistischen Reife aus: charakteristisch ist die extreme Streckung der Körper / Expose les premières œuvres de la maturité stylistique, caractérisées par l'extrême allongement des corps / Toont de eerste werken van zijn stylistische rijpheid, gekarakteriseerd door extreem uitgerekte lichamen
1951 Paris, Aimé Maeght Gallery: First exhibition of sculpture and painting / Erste Ausstellung von Skulpturen und Bildern / Première exposition de sculptures et peintures / Eerste beeldhouwwerken-en schilderijententoonstelling
1962 Venezia: Won Gran premio for sculpture at Biennale / Großer Preis für Bildhauerei auf der Biennale / Lauréat du grand prix de sculpture à la Biennale / Wint de Grote Prijs van de Beeldhouwkunst tijdens de Biënnale
1964 Guggenheim prize for painting / Gran Prix Guggenheim für Malerei / Grand prix Guggenheim de peinture / Guggenheim Grote Prijs voor de Schilderkunst
Began work on busts of Elie Lotar / Er beginnt an den Büsten von Elie Lotar zu arbeiten / Commence à travailler aux bustes d'Elie Lotar / Begint met het werken aan de bustes van Elie Lotar
1966 Zurich: The Alberto Giacometti Foundation inaugurated at the Kunsthaus / Es wird die Alberto Giacometti-Stiftung im Kunsthaus eröffnet / Inauguration de la Fondation Alberto Giacometti à la Kunsthaus / Het Alberto Giacometti Fonds wordt in het Kunsthaus geopend

---

Barbara Hepworth
Wakefield 1903 - St. Ives 1975
1920-1923 London: Studied at the Leeds School of Art, and at the Royal College of Art, where she met Henry Moore / Studien an der Leeds School of Art, dann am Royal College, wo sie Henry Moore kennenlernt / Études à la Leeds School of Art, puis au Royal College. Y fait la connaissance d'Henry Moore / Studeert aan de Leeds School of Art, daarna aan het Royal College, waar ze Henry Moore leert kennen
1924 Prix de Rome
1924-1925 Travels in Italy: Florence, Siena, Rome / Dann Italienreise: Florenz, Siena, Rom / Part pour l'Italie: Florence, Sienne, Rome / Reist vervolgens naar Italië: Florence, Sienna en Rome
1925-1926 Roma: began sculpting in marble / Beginnt sie Marmor zu bearbeiten / Se lance dans la sculpture du marbre / Begint met het bewerken van marmer
1927-1931 London, Glasgow: Sculpture exhibitions / Sie stellt ihre Skulpturen / Expose ses sculptures / Toont haar beeldhouwwerken
1930-1931 In the London Group with Moore and in the Seven and Five Society (7 painters and 5 sculptors engaged in abstract research) / Nimmt mit Moore an der London Group und an der 7 & 5 Society teil / Participe avec Moore au *London Group* et à la *7&5 Society* / Neemt met Moore deel aan de London Group en de 7 & 5 Society
1932 Travelled in France with Ben Nicholson: visits to Brancusi, Arp, Braque, Picasso / Frankreichreise mit Ben Nicholson; zusammen besuchen sie Brancusi, Arp, Braque und Picasso / Voyage en France avec Ben Nicholson. Rendent visite, ensemble, à Brancusi, Arp, Braque, Picasso / Reist

naar Frankrijk met Ben Nicholson. Samen bezoeken ze Brâncuşi, Arp, Braque en Picasso Engaged with the *Abstraction-Création* group / Sie schließt sich der Gruppe *Abstraction-Création* an / Adhère au groupe *Abstraction-Création* / Sluit zich aan bij de groep *Abstraction-Création*

1939-1942 St. Ives, Cornwall: Worked in ceramic and metal / Hier arbeitet sie mit Keramik und Metall / Travaille la céramique et le métal / Bewerkt daar keramiek en metaal

1943 Temple Newsman, Leeds: First personal show / Erste Einzelausstellung / Première exposition personnelle / Eerste persoonlijke tentoonstelling

1949-1953 Exhibited at Venice Biennale. Two retrospectives in Wakenfield and London. Herbert Read (1952) wrote monograph / Teilnahme an der Biennale in Venedig; zwei Retrospektiven in Wakenfield und in London. Herausgabe der Monographie von Herbert Read (1952) / Participe à la Biennale de Venise. Deux rétrospectives à Wakefield et à Londres. Publie la monographie d'Herbert Read (1952) / Neemt deel aan de Biënnale van Venetië. Twee retrospectieve tentoonstellingen in Wakenfield en in Londen. De monografie over Herbert Read (1952) wordt gepubliceerd

1954 Greece / Griechenlandbesuch / Grèce / Griekenland

1959 Won Gran Premio for sculpture at the São Paulo Art Biennial / Großer Preis für Bildhauerei auf der Biennale von São Paolo in Brasilien / Remporte le grand prix de sculpture à la Biennale de Saõ Paulo, Brésil / Wint de Grote Prijs voor de Beeldhouwkunst tijdens de Biënnale van Sao Paolo van Brazilië

1975 Ill with cancer, she died following a fire in her studio / Nach langem Kampf gegen einen Tumor stirbt sie schließlich bei einem Brand / Après une longue lutte contre le cancer, meurt dans un incendie / Komt, na een lange strijd tegen een tumor, bij een brand om het leven

1976 Her studio and house became the Barbara Hepworth Museum, from 1980 part of the Tate. Tate St. Ives was opened in 1993 / Atelier und Haus werden zum Barbara Hepworth Museum, das ab 1980 in den Besitz der Tate übergeht. Tate St. Ives wurde 1993 eröffnet / Son atelier et sa maison deviennent le Barbara Hepworth Museum qui, depuis 1980, appartient à la Tate Gallery Ouverture en 1953 de la Tate St. Ives / Het atelier en het huis worden het Barbara Hepworth Museum, dat in 1980 eigendom wordt van Tate. Tate St. Ives wordt geopend in 1993

Frida Kahlo
Coyoacán, Ciudad de México 1907 - 1954

1910-1920 Frida asserted that she was the daughter of German Jewish immigrants. Her childhood was very troubled / Tochter eines deutsch-jüdischen Emigranten; sie wird in der Jugendzeit schwer heimgesucht / Fille d'un émigré juif allemand, vit une jeunesse tourmentée / Dochter van een Hebreeuws-Duitse immigrant, leidt een pijnlijke jeugd

1929 Married Mexican painter Diego Rivera / Hochzeit mit dem mexikanischen Maler Diego Rivera / Épouse le peintre mexicain Diego Rivera / Trouwt met de Mexicaanse schilder Diego Rivera

1938 New York: Important show / Wichtige anthologische Ausstellung / Importante exposition anthologique / Belangrijke anthologische tentoonstelling

1939 Paris: Photography exhibition organized by the Surrealists: introduced to group by Duchamp / Monographische Ausstellung, organisiert von den Surrealisten; Durch die Vermittlung Duchamp wird sie deren Freundin / Exposition monographique organisée par les surréalistes dont elle devient l'amie par l'intermédiaire de Duchamp / Monografische tentoonstelling georganiseerd door surrealisten, met wie zij via Duchamp bevriend raakt

1953 Ciudad de México: Major exhibtion / Wichtige anthologische Ausstellung / Exposition anthologique / Belangrijke anthologische tentoonstelling

René Magritte
Lessen 1898 - Brussel 1967

1912   Mother's suicide, impact on his painting / Selbstmord der Mutter, der die Malerei des Künstlers prägt / Suicide de sa mère, qui marquera à jamais sa peinture / Zelfmoord van zijn moeder, wat vaak terugkeert in de werken van de kunstenaar

1925   Brussel: Joined surrealist group / Er schließt sich den Surrealisten / Adhésion au groupe surréaliste / Sluit zich aan bij de surrealisten

1926   Contact with André Breton / Kontaktaufnahme mit André Breton / Entre en contact avec André Breton / Raakt in contact met André Breton

1928   Moved near Paris. Friendship with Joan Miró, Paul Éluard and Jean (Hans) Arp / Er zieht in die Nähe von Paris und schließt Freundschaft mit Joan Miró, Paul Éluard und Jean (Hans) Arp / S'installe dans les environs de Paris. Se lie d'amitié avec Joan Miró, Paul Eluard et Jean (Hans) Arp / Verhuist naar de omgeving van Parijs, raakt bevriend met Joan Miró, Paul Éluard en Jean (Hans) Arp

1929   Cadaqués: Stayed with Dalí with Paul and Gala Éluard / Gast bei Dalí mit Paul und Gala Éluard / Est l'hôte de Dali en même temps que Paul Eluard et Gala / Is met Paul en Gala Éluard gast van Dalí; *Les Mots et les images* for the *Révolution surréaliste*
La Trahison des images (Ceci n'est pas une pipe) (County Museum of Art, Los Angeles)

1930   Returned to Belgium and started advertising agency / Rückkehr nach Belgien und Beginn seiner Tätigkeit als Werbefachmann / Rentre en Belgique et se lance dans la publicité / Keert terug naar België en begint voor zichzelf als reclamemaker

1936   New York, Julien Lévy Gallery: Took part in surrealist collective / Er stellt mit anderen Künstlern auf der surrealistischen Ausstellung aus / Se trouve parmi les exposants de l'exposition collective surréaliste / Is één van de exposanten bij de collectieve tentoonstelling van surrealisten

1940-1957   Developed a witty surrealist style extremely influential on younger generations / Es reift sein essenzieller, effektvoller Stil, der lange Zeit auf die jungen Generationen Einfluss haben wird / Affirme de plus en plus son style, essentiel, efficace, qui influencera les jeunes générations / Ontwikkelt een essentiële, levensechte stijl, die grote invloed zou hebben op de nieuwe generatie

1957   *La Fée ignorante* (Palais des Beaux-Arts, Charleroi)

André Masson
Balagny-sur-Thérain 1896 - Paris 1987

1915-1923   Adopted a cubist style after the war / Nach dem Krieg malt er in kubistischem Stil / Après la guerre, peint dans un style cubiste / Schildert na de oorlog in kubistische stijl
Met Breton and the Surrealists / Er nimmt Kontakt zu Breton und den Surrealisten auf / Entre en contact avec Breton et les surréalistes / Raakt in contact met Breton en de surrealisten

1925   Paris, Galerie Pierre: Exhibited in the first surreal exhibition / Teilnahme an Ausstellung der Surrealisten / Participe à la première exposition des surréalistes / Exposeert tijdens de Eerste Tentoonstelling van de Surrealisten.
Cadavres exquises

1929   Broke with André Breton / Bruch mit André Breton / Rompt avec André Breton / Breekt met André Breton
Joined dissident surrealist circle / Er schließt sich dem Kreis der surrealistischen Dissidenten an / Entre dans le cercle des surréalistes dissidents / Begeeft zich in de kringen van de dissidente surrealisten

1940   Moved to the U.S.A: influential in development of the New York School / Umzug in die Vereinigten Staaten, wo er ein wichtiges Beispiel für die Entwicklung der New York School wird / S'installe à New York où il devient un modèle important pour le développement de la New York School / Verhuist naar de Verenigde Saten, waar hij een belangrijk voorbeeld voor de ontwikkeling van de New York School wordt

Roberto Sebastian Matta
Santiago de Chile 1911 - Civitavecchia 2002
- 1920 Studied architecture in Chile / Architekturstudien in Chile / Études d'architecture au Chili / Studeert architectuur in Chili
- 1934-1939 Paris: Worked in Le Corbusier's studio. Frequented Surrealists / Arbeitet er im Atelier von Le Corbusier, lernt di Surrealisten kennen und frequentiert sie / Travaille à l'agence de Le Corbusier. Fait la connaissance des surréalistes et les fréquente / Werkt in het atelier van Le Corbusier. Leert de surrealisten kennen en bezoekt ze regelmatig
- 1940 New York: Strong influence on young Jackson Pollock and Arshile Gorky / Übt er starken Einfluss auf junge Künstler wie Jackson Pollock und Arshile Gorkij aus / Exerce une forte influence sur les jeunes comme Jackson Pollock et Arshile Gorky / Oefent een grote invloed uit op jongeren als Jackson Pollock en Arshile Gorkij
- 1949 Rome
- 1954 Paris
- 1960 Buys ex-convent of Passionist friars in Tarquinia / Tarquinia wird zu seinem zweiten Wohnort, wo er in ein ehemaliges Passionistenkloster zieht / Choisit Tarquinia comme résidence secondaire et s'installe dans un ancien couvent de moines passionnistes / Kiest Tarquinia als zijn tweede woonplaats, zich vestigend in een voormalig klooster van de Frati Passionisti
- 1974-1976 *Autoapocalipse*
- 1985 Centre Georges Pompidou, Paris: Major retrospective / Bedeutende Retrospektive / Grande rétrospective / grote retrospectieve tentoonstelling

Joan Miró
Barcelona 1893 - Palma de Mallorca 1983
- 1919-1926 Barcelona: Attended Francisco Galí art school / Besuch der Kunstschule von Francisco Galí / Fréquente l'École d'Art de Francisco Gali / Bezoekt de Kunstschool van Francisco Galí
  Paris: Met Picasso and joined surrealist group / Lernt er Picasso kennen und schließt sich der Gruppe der Surrealisten an / Fait la connaissance de Picasso et adhère au groupe surréaliste / Leert Picasso kennen en sluit zich aan bij de surrealisten
  Met Arp and Ernst: Experimented new painting techniques / Mit Arp und Ernst experimentiert er an neuen Maltechniken / Avec Arp et Ernst, expérimente de nouvelles techniques de peinture / Experimenteert met nieuwe schildertechnieken met Arp en Ernst
- 1928 Travels in Belgium and Low Countries inspiration for *Dutch Interiors* / Reise nach Belgien und in die Niederlande, wo die Serie Holländisches Interieur entsteht / Entreprend un voyage en Belgique et aux Pays-Bas où il peint la série des *Intérieurs hollandais* / Onderneemt een reis naar België en naar Nederland, waar de serie *Hollands Interieur* ontstaat
- 1930 Paris, Galerie Goemans: Took part in the *collages* exhibition / Teilnahme an der großen *Collage* Ausstellung / Participe à la grande exposition consacrée aux *collages* / Neemt deel aan de grote tentoonstelling, gewijd aan *collages*
- 1932-1936 Barcelona: Met Josep Lluís Sert / Er trifft Josep Lluís Sert / Rencontre Josep Lluis Sert / Waar hij Joseph Lluís Sert ontmoet
- 1939 Varengeville-sur-Mer, Normandie
- 1940 Returned to Spain after German invasion / Anlässlich der deutschen Invasion in Frankreich, kehrt er nach Spanien zurück / Pendant l'Occupation de la France, retourne en Espagne / Keert, door de Duitse invasie van Frankrijk, terug naar Spanje
- 1941 Museum of Modern Art, New York: Major retrospective / Wichtige Retrospektive / Importante exposition rétrospective / Belangrijke retrospectieve tentoonstelling
  Began working in ceramics and bronze sculpture / Beginn seiner Keramikarbeiten und Bronzeskulpturen / Se consacre à des travaux de céramique et de sculpture en bronze / Begint zich toe te leggen op keramiekwerken en bronssculpturen
- 1954 Venezia: Prize for graphics at Biennale / Preis für Graphik anlässlich der Biennale / Gagne le prix

de graphisme à la Biennale / Wint de prijs voor de grafische kunst tijdens de Biënnale
1956 Palma de Mallorca
1958 Paris: *Wall of the Moon* and *Wall of the Sun* for UNESCO building / Skulpturen die *Mauer des Mondes* und die *Mauer der Sonne* für das UNESCO Gebäude / Réalise les sculptures le *Mur de la Lune* et le *Mur du Soleil* pour l'Unesco / Verwezenlijkt de beeldhouwwerken *Le Mur de la Lune* en *Le mur du Soleil* in het Unescogebouw
1978 Monumental sculptures. *Woman and bird* mural in the Joan Miró park in Barcellona / Er widmet sich der monumentalen Skulptur: auf diese Zeit geht seine berühmte Skulptur *Frau und Vogel* im Joan Miró-Park in Barcelona zurück / Se consacre à la sculpture monumentale. *Femme et Oiseau*, sa célèbre sculpture située dans le parc Joan Miró de Barcelone, remonte à cette époque / Legt zich toe op monumentale beeldhouwwerken. Wordt in deze periode bekend door zijn gevierde beeldhouwwerk *Vrouw en Vogel* in het Joan Miró Park in Barcelona

---

Henry Moore
Castleford 1898 - Much Hadham 1986
1919-1924 London: Studied at Leeds School of Art and Royal College of Art / Studien der Bildhauerei an der Leeds School of Art, dann an der Royal College / Étudie la sculpture à la School of Art de Leeds, puis au Royal College of Art / Studeert beeldhouwkunst aan de Leeds School of Art, studeert daarna aan het Royal College
1923 Paris
1925 Six months in Italy, studied old masters from Middle Ages to the Renaissance / Auf seiner sechs Monate langen Reise in Italien studiert er die Großen Meister des Mittelalters und der Renaissance / Séjourne six mois en Italie et étudie les grands maîtres du Moyen Âge et de la Renaissance / Verblijft zes maanden in Italië, om de grote meesters van de Middeleeuwen en de Renaissance te bestuderen
1926-1935 London: Began teaching sculpture at Royal College of Art / Widmet er sich dem Bildhauereiunterricht in der Royal College of Art / Se consacre à l'enseignement de la sculpture au Royal College of Art / Keert terug naar Londen en wijdt zich aan het onderwijzen van beeldhouwkunst aan het Royal College of Art
London, Warren Gallery: First one-man show / Erste Einzelausstellung / Première exposition personnelle / Eerste persoonlijke tentoonstelling
Involved in the Seven & Five Society (7 painters and 5 sculptors engaged in abstract research) / Er nimmt an den Aktivitäten der Seven & Five Society teil, die aus sieben Malern und fünf Bildhauern besteht und sich mit der abstrakten Kunst beschäftigt / Participe aux travaux de la Seven & Five Society, où sept peintres et cinq sculpteurs sont engagés dans la recherche sur l'abstrait / Neemt deel aan de activiteiten van de Seven & Five Society, groep van zeven schilders en vijf beeldhouwers, die zich toelegden op de zoektocht naar de abstracte kunst
1936 London: Signed manifesto of English surrealist group and took part in the *International Surrealist Exhibition* at the New Burlington Galleries / Er unterschreibt das Manifest der englischen Surrealisten und nimmt im gleichen Jahr an der *International Surrealist Exhibition* teil, die in den New Burlington Galleries stattfindet / Signe le manifeste du groupe surréaliste anglais et participe cette année-là à l'exposition surréaliste internationale aux New Burlington Galleries / Ondertekent het manifest van de Engelse surrealisten en neemt in hetzelfde jaar deel aan de *International Surrealist Exhibition*, gehouden in de New Burlington Galleries
1941 Perry Green, Hertfordshire
1946 Museum of Modern Art, New York: First major retrospective abroad / Eröffnung der ersten großen Retrospektive im Ausland / Inauguration de la première grande rétrospective à l'étranger / Opent zijn eerste grote retrospectieve tentoonstelling in het buitenland
1951 Tours classical Greece / Besuch des Klassischen Griechenland / Visite la Grèce classique / Bezoekt het Oude Griekenland
1952 Award at the São Paulo Biennial in Brasil / Preis anlässlich der II. Biennale von São Paolo in

Brasilien / Primé à la deuxième Biennale de Saõ Paulo, au Brésil / Wint prijs tijdens de Biënnale van San Paolo van Brazilië
1956-1966 Tuscany / Toskana / Toscane
Worked in marble workshops at Carrara and Pietrasanta / Marmorarbeiten in den Werkstätten von Carrara und Pietrasanta / Travaille le marbre dans les laboratoires de Carrare et Pietrasanta / Bewerkt marmer in de Werkplaatsen van Carrara en Pietrasanta
1972 Florence, Forte Belvedere: Major exhibtion / Große anthologische Ausstellung / Grande exposition anthologique / Grote anthologische tentoonstelling
Founded Henry Moore Trust, administered by the Tate Gallery / Er gründet den Henry Moore Trust, der von der Tate Gallery verwaltet wird / Fonde l'Henry Moore Trust, administré par la Tate Gallery / Sticht het Henry Moore Trust, beheerd door Tate Gallery
1976 Henry Moore Foundation created / Er gründet die Henry Moore Foundation / Crée la fondation Henry Moore / Sticht de Henry Moore Foundation
1982 Queen Elizabeth II of England opens the Henry Moore Sculpture Gallery and Centre for the Study of Sculpture / Königin Elisabeth II. eröffnet offiziell die Henry Moore Sculpture Gallery und das Centre for the Study of Sculpture / La reine Elisabeth II inaugure officiellement la Henry Moore Sculpture Gallery et le Centre for the Study of Sculpture / Koningin Elizabeth II opent officieel de Henry Moore Sculpture Gallery and Centre for the Study of Sculpture
1983 New York, Metropolitan Museum of Art: Major retrospective / Wichtige Retrospektive / Importante rétrospective / Houdt een belangrijke retrospectieve tentoonstelling
1984 Left property at Perry Green and his entire collection to Henry Moore Foundation / Der gesamte Besitz von Perry Green einschließlich seiner eigenen Kollektion gehen an die gleichnamige Stiftung / Cède toute la propriété de Perry Green y compris sa collection personnelle, à sa Fondation / Laat al zijn bezittingen in Perry Green, met zijn collectie na aan de gelijknamige Foundation

Meret Oppenheim
Berlin 1913 - Basel 1985
1932 Studied in Germany and Switzerland / Studien in Deutschland und in der Schweiz / Étudie en Allemagne et en Suisse / Studeert in Duitsland en in Zwitserland
1932 Paris: With Irène Zurkinden / Mit ihrer Freundin Irène Zurkinde / Séjourne avec son amie Irène Zurkinde / Met haar vriendin Irène Zurkinde
1932-1939 Paris: Contact with Arp, Giacometti, Man Ray / Frequentiert sie Arp, Giacometti und Man Ray / Fréquente Arp, Giacometti, Man Ray / Bezoekt regelmatig Arp, Giacometti en Man Ray
1936 Déjeuner en fourrure (Museum of Modern Art, New York)
Drawn to Surrealism / Sie schließt sich dem Surrealismus an / Adhère au surréalisme / Sluit zich aan bij het Surrealisme
1939 Bern
1975 Art Award, City of Basel / Kunstpreis der Stadt Basel / Lauréate du prix d'Art de la ville de Bâle / Kunstprijs van de stad Bazel
1982 Grand Art Prize, City of Berlin / Großer Preis der Stadt Berlin / Grand prix de la ville de Berlin / Grote Kunstprijs van de stad Berlijn

Francis Picabia
Paris 1879 - 1953
1895 Paris: Studied at the École des Arts Décoratifs / Studien an der École des Arts Décoratifs / Études à l'École des arts décoratifs / Studeert aan de École des Arts Décoratifs
1910-1912 Influenced by Cubism, moved increasingly towards abstract expression / Unter dem Einfluss des Kubismus, nähert er sich immer mehr dem abstrakten Bild / Influencé par le cubisme, se

rapproche de plus en plus de l'abstrait / Beïnvloed door het Kubisme, neigt hij steeds verder naar abstracte afbeeldingen

1913 New York: In the circle of Alfred Stieglitz and exhibited at the 291 gallery / Er frequentiert den Zirkel von Alfred Stieglitz und stellt in der Galerie 291 aus / Fréquente le cercle d'Alfred Stieglitz et expose à la galerie 291 / Bezoekt regelmatig de club van Alfred Stieglitz en exposeert in galerie 291

1915 First mechanical paintings / Erste Bilder mit Maschinen und Räderwerken / Réalise les premières peintures avec machines et engrenages / Verwezenlijkt het eerste schilderij met machines en tandwielen

1917 Barcelona: Founded the Dada *391* periodical / Gründung der Zeitschrift *391*/ Fonde la revue *391* / Richt het tijdschrift *391* op

1919 Zurich: Cabaret Voltaire
Lived and worked in Paris ; frequented first Dadaists and then Surrealists / Er lebt und arbeitet in Paris: Dada, dann Surrealist / Vit et travaille à Paris dans le milieu dada, puis surréaliste / Woont en werkt in Parijs in de kringen van de Dadaïsten en daarna in die van de Surrealisten

1921 Salon d'Automne, Paris : *L'Oeil Cacodylate* (Musée National d'Art Moderne, Paris)

Pablo Picasso
Málaga 1881 - Mougins 1973

1900-1901 Paris
Suicide of friend Carlos Casagemas marks beginning of blue period / In Folge des Selbstmordes seines spanischen Freundes Carlos Casagemas beginnt seine Blaue Periode / Après le suicide de son ami espagnol Carlos Casagemas, inaugure la période bleue / Luidt, als gevolg van de zelfmoord van zijn Spaanse vriend Carlos Casagemas, de Blauwe periode

1904 Paris

1905-1906 Rose period / Rosa Periode / Période rose / Roze Periode

1907 *Les Demoiselles d'Avignon* (Museum of Modern Art, New York)

1910-1912 Analytical Cubism / Es beginnt die Periode seines analytischen Kubismus / Début de la période du cubisme analytique / Begint met de fase van het analytische Kubisme

1912-1917 Synthetic Cubism and experimentation with *collages* / Beginn des synthetischen Kubismus und Experimente mit den ersten *Collages* / Ouvre la voie au cubisme synthétique et tente les premiers collages / Begint met het synthetische Kubisme en experimenteert met de eerste *collages*

1917-1927 Italy / Italienreise / Italie / Italië
Collaboration with Ballets Russes / Arbeiten mit dem russischen Ballett / Collabore aux ballets russes / Werkt mee aan het Russisch Ballet
Approached surrealism / Er nähert sich dem Surrealismus / Se rapproche du surréalisme / Sluit zich aan bij het Realisme

1928-1929 Experimentation with iron sculpture wih Julio Gonzales / Gemeinsam mit seinem Freund Julio Gonzales experimentiert er mit Eisenskulpturen / Expérimente la sculpture en fer avec son ami Julio Gonzales / Experimenteert met beeldhouwwerken van ijzer met zijn vriend Julio Gonzales

1930-1938 Purchased chateau at Boisgeloup and studio on rue des Grands-Augustins, in Paris where he painted *Guernica* / Er kauft das Schloss von Boisgeloup und in Paris das Atelier in der rue des Grands-Augustins, wo er *Guernica* malt / Achète le château de Boisgeloup et à Paris l'atelier de la rue des Grands-Augustins, où il peint *Guernica* / Koopt het Kasteel Boisgeloup en in Parijs het atelier aan de rue des Grand-Augustins, waar hij *Guernica* schildert

1947-1948 A Vallauris on the Cote d'Azure works in ceramics at the Madoura factory / In Vallauris an der Côte d'Azur beschäftigt er sich mit Keramik in der Madoura Fabrik / À Vallauris, sur la Côte d'Azur, expérimente la céramique à la fabrique Madoura / Experimenteert met keramiek in Vallauris aan de Côte d'Azur in de Madoura fabriek

1955 La California, Cannes
1958 Inauguration of *The fall of Icarus* for the UNESCO centre in Paris / Wandgemälde *Der Sturz des Ikarus* für das UNESCO Gebäude in Paris / Inauguration de *La Chute d'Icare* pour le palais de l'Unesco, à Paris / Inwijding van *De val van Icarus* voor het Unescogebouw in Parijs
1963 Barcelona: Picasso Museum opened / Eröffnung des Picasso Museums / Ouverture du musée Picasso / Opent het Picasso Museum
1966 Paris, Grand Palais en Petit Palais: Major retrospective exhibition / Große Retrospektive / Dragen een grote retrospectieve tentoonstelling aan hem op / Une grande exposition rétrospective lui est consacrée

Man Ray
Philadephia 1890 - Paris 1976
1912 New York: Followed the courses at the Modern School, with the leaders of radical avant-garde / Besucht er die Kurse der Modern School mit den Protagonisten der radikalen avantgardistischen Kulturszene / Suit les cours de la Modern School, avec les protagonistes de la culture d'avant-garde radicale / Volgt lessen aan de Modern School met de protagonisten van de radicale avantgardistische cultuur
1913 Visited the Armory Show, struck by the European avant-garde / Er besucht die Armory Show und ist von den Werken der europäischen Avantgarde beeindruckt / Visite l'Armory Show. Est impressionné par les œuvres de l'avant-garde européenne / Bezoekt de Armory Show, raakt diep onder de indruk van de werken van de Europese avant-garde
1916 *The Rope Dancer accompanies Herself with her Shadows* (Museum of Modern Art, New York)
1921 With Duchamp published *New York Dada* magazine / Er publiziert mit Duchamp die Zeitschrift *New York Dada* / Publie avec Marcel Duchamp la revue *New York Dada* / Publiceert samen met Duchamp het tijdschrift *New York Dada*
1922 Experiments with photographic techiniques: *Rayograms* / Anhand seiner neuen Technik des direkten Ablichtens von Negativen erzeugt er die *Rayogramme* / Travaille à une nouvelle technique d'impression directe du négatif et produit des *Rayogrammes* / Werkt aan een nieuwe directe afdruktechniek van het negatief en produceert *Rayogrammen*
Closer to Surrealists / Er schließt sich dem Surrealismus an / Se rapproche du milieu surréaliste / Begeeft zich in de wereld van de surrealisten
1923-1929 Experimental films: *Anémic Cinéma* with Duchamp / Verschiedene Experimentalfilme, darunter *Anémic Cinéma* mit Duchamp / Tourne divers films expérimentaux, parmi lesquels *Anemic Cinéma* avec Duchamp / Neemt verschillende experimentele films op, waaronder *Anémic Cinéma* met Duchamp
1940 Returned to United States at outbreak of war / Bei Kriegsausbruch kehrt er in die Vereinigten Staaten zurück / Rentre aux États-Unis quand la guerre éclate / Keert terug naar de Verenigde Staten na het uitbreken van de oorlog

Alberto Savinio
Athína 1891 - Roma 1952
1895-1905 Childhood in Vólos in Greece / Kindheit in Vólos, Griechenland / Enfance à Vólos, en Grèce / Jeugd in Vólos in Griekenland
1910 Began literary activity / Literarische Tätigkeit / Se consacre à la littérature / Wijdt zich aan literaire activiteiten
1925-1926 Turned to painting: continued writing in surrealist vein / Er beginnt zu malen, darüber hinaus surrealistisch inspirierte Schriften / Se lance dans la peinture tout en écrivant, inspiré par le surréalisme / Begint, geïnspireerd door de surrealisten, naast het schrijven, met het schilderen

1929 *La sposa fedele* / *Die treue Braut* / *L'Épouse fidèle* / *La fidèle épouse* (Galleria dello Scudo, Verona)

1948 Directed, designed costumes and sets for *Oedipus Rex* by Stravinsky at the Scala in Milan: text by Jean Cocteau / Theaterarbeiten: an der Mailänder Scala kümmert er sich um Regie, Bühnenbild und Kostüme des *Oedipus Rex* von Stravinskij, mit Texten von Jean Cocteau / Activité théâtrale : à la Scala de Milan, assure la régie, la mise en scène et les costumes d'*Œdipus Rex* (Œdipe-roi) de Stravinski, avec des textes de Jean Cocteau / Theateractiviteiten: draagt bij La Scala in Milaan zorg voor de regie, de scènes en de kostuums van *Oedipus Rex* van Stravinsky, geschreven door Jean Cocteau

---

Yves Tanguy
Paris 1900 - Woodburg, CT. 1955

1922 Paris: He chanced to see paintings of Giorgio de Chirico and decided to become a painter / Entdeckt er seine Leidenschaft für die Malerei und beginnt Szenen aus dem Kaffeehausleben zu zeichnen / Découvre sa passion pour la peinture en commençant à dessiner des scènes de vie au café / Ontdekt zijn passie voor de schilderkunst en begint met het tekenen van caféscènes

1923-1925 Er hat die Gelegenheit, Bilder Giorgio De Chirico zu sehen und beschließt, Maler zu werden / Voit les tableaux de Giorgio De Chirico et décide de devenir peintre / Krijgt de kans schilderijen van Giorgio De Chirico te bekijken en besluit schilder te worden

André Breton introduces him to the surrealist group / Er wird von André Breton in die surrealistische Gruppe eingeführt / André Breton l'introduit parmi les membres du groupe surréaliste / Wordt door André Breton voorgesteld aan de leden van de surrealistengroep

1927 Paris, Galerie Surréaliste: First one-man show / Erste Einzelausstellung / Première exposition personnelle / Eerste persoonlijke tentoonstelling

1942 New York, Pierre Matisse Gallery: Took part in *Artists in Exile* exhibition; his work was frequently on show until 1950 / Er nimmt an der Ausstellung *Artists in Exile;* wo er bis 1950 regelmäßig ausstellt / Participe à l'exposition «Artists in exile»; il expose fréquemment jusqu'en 1950 / Neemt deel aan de tentoonstelling *Artists in Exile*, waar hij tot aan 1950 regelmatig exposeert

1947 Saint-Paul de Vence, Galerie Maeght: Included in the surrealist exhibition organised by André Breton and Marcel Duchamp / Er stellt auf der Ausstellung der Surrealisten aus, die von Breton und Marcel Duchamp organisiert ist / Participe à l'exposition des surréalistes organisée par André Breton et Marcel Duchamp / Exposeert op de tentoonstelling van de surrealisten, georganiseerd door Breton en Marcel Duchamp

1948 Became a United States citizen / Er beschließt, die amerikanische Staatsbürgerschaft anzunehmen / Décide de prendre la nationalité américaine / Besluit het Amerikaanse staatsburgerschap aan te nemen

1955 New York, Museum of Modern Art: Eight months after his death major retrospective / Acht Monate nach seinem Tod wird eine Retrospektive des Künstlers gezeigt / Huit mois après sa mort, une grande rétrospective lui est consacrée / Acht maanden na zijn dood zal er een retrospectieve tentoonstelling over de kunstenaar worden georganiseerd

Museums and Galleries of Surrealist Art
Die museen Surrealistischer kunst
Les musées d'art Surréaliste
Musea voor de Surrealistische kunst

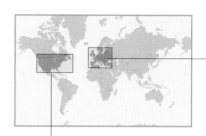

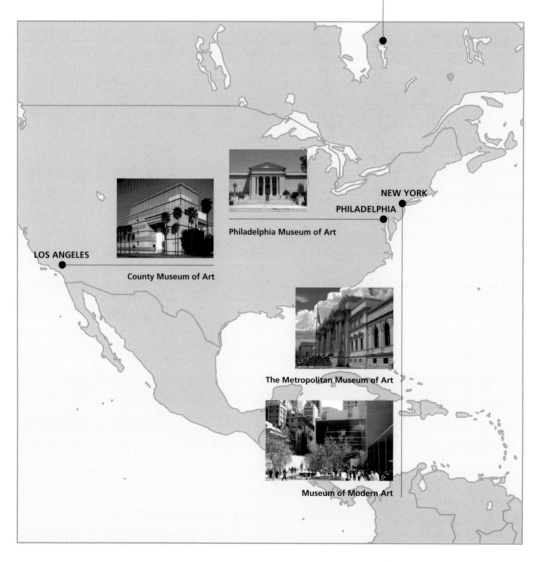

NEW YORK

PHILADELPHIA

Philadelphia Museum of Art

LOS ANGELES

County Museum of Art

The Metropolitan Museum of Art

Museum of Modern Art

Hamburger Kunsthalle

René Magritte Museum

Nationalgalerie

HAMBURG

BERLIN

BRUSSEL

Centre Georges Pompidou - Musée
National d'Art Moderne

PARIS

Collezione Peggy Guggenheim

VENEZIA

MADRID

Museo Thyssen-Bornemisza

© 2011 SCALA Group S.p.A.
62, via Chiantigiana
50012 Bagno a Ripoli
Florence (Italy)

Text and picture research: Giovanna Uzzani

English translation: Heather Mackay Roberts
French translation: Denis-Armand Canal

Printed in China 2011

ISBN (English): 978-88-6637-079-6
ISBN (German): 978-88-6637-078-9
ISBN (Dutch): 978-88-6637-080-2

Created and distributed in cooperation with Frechmann Kolón GmbH
www.frechmann.com

Project Management: E-ducation.it S.p.A. Firenze

Picture credits
© 2011 Archivio Scala, Firenze:
© Digital image, The Museum of Modern Art, New York/Scala, Florence, © Image copyright The Metropolitan Museum of Art/Art Resource/Scala, Florence, © Photo Scala, Florence/BPK, Bildagentur fuer Kunst, Kultur und Geschichte, Berlin, © White Images/Scala, Florence,© BI, ADAGP, Paris/Scala, Florence, © Foto Schalkwijk/Art Resource/Scala, Firenze, © Foto Art Resource/Scala, Firenze, © Foto The Philadelphia Museum of Art/Art Resource/Scala, Firenze, © Yale University Art Gallery/Art Resource, NY/Scala, Firenze, © Kimbell Art Museum, Fort Worth, Texas /Art Resource, NY/Scala, Firenze, © Foto Smithsonian American Art Museum/Art Resource/ Scala, Firenze.
Maps: Geoatlas

© Copyright by SIAE 2011 for the following authors:
Jean (Hans) Arp, Balthus, Hans Bellmer, Victor Brauner, Andrè Breton, Giorgio De Chirico, Max Ernst, Valentine Hugo, Wilfredo Lam, Renè Magritte, Andrè Masson, Roberto Sebastian Matta Echaurren, Max Morise, Meret Oppenheim, Francis Picabia, Alberto Savinio, Yves Tanguy

Joseph Cornell: © The Joseph and Robert Cornell Memorial Foundation, by SIAE 2011
Salvador Dalí: © Salvador Dalí, Gala-Salvador Dalí Foundation, by SIAE 2011
Paul Delvaux: © Paul Delvaux Fondation, by SIAE 2011
Marcel Duchamp: © Succession Marcel Duchamp, by SIAE 2011
Frida Kahlo: © Banco del México Diego Rivera & Frida Kahlo Museums Trust, México D.F, by SIAE 2011
Alberto Giacometti © Fondation Alberto et Annette Giacometti, by SIAE 2011
Joan Miró: © Successió Miró - by SIAE 2011
Pablo Picasso: © Succession Picasso, by SIAE 2011

Man Ray: © Man Ray Trust, by SIAE 2011
Horst P. Horst : © Horst P. Horst / Art + Commerce
Henry Moore: © Henry Moore Foundation
Paul and Nush Eluard: © Archivio Scala

The SCALA images reproducing artworks that belong to the Italian State are published with the permission of the Ministry for Cultural Heritage and Activities.

Every effort has been made to trace all copyright owners, but if any have been inadvertently overlooked, the Publishers will be pleased to make the necessary arrangements at the first opportunity.

Appendix to image credits:
THE METROPOLITAN MUSEUM OF ART, NEW YORK
Brauner Victor, Prelude to a Civilization, 1954, encaustic, and pen and ink on Masonite, H. 51, W. 79-3/4 inches (129.5 x 202.5 cm.).Jacques and Natasha Gelman Collection, 1998. Acc.n.: 1999.363.13.Photo: Malcom Varon; Dali' Salvador, Madonna, 1958, oil on canvas, H. 88-7/8, W. 75-1/4 inches (225.7 x 191.1 cm.). Gift of Drue Heinz, in memory of Henry J. Heinz II, 1987. Acc.n.: 1987.465; Giacometti Alberto, Three Men Walking (II), 1949, bronze, 30 1/8 x 13 x 12 3/4 in. (76.5 x 33 x 32.4 cm.).Jacques and Natasha Gelman Collection, 1998. Acc.n.: 1999.363.22.Photo: Malcolm Varon; Miro' Joan, Animated Landscape, 1927, oil on canvas, H. 51, W. 76-3/4 inches (129.5 x 195 cm.). Jacques and Natasha Gelman Collection, 1998. Acc.n.: 1999.363.49.Photo: Malcom Varon; Picasso Pablo, Nude Standing by the Sea, 1929, oil on canvas, 51 1/8 x 38 1/8 in. (129.9 x 96.8 cm). Inscribed: L.L.: ¦Picasso¦/29.Bequest of Florene M. Schoenborn, 1995. Acc.n.: 1996.403.4; Picasso Pablo, Faun and Starry Night, 1955, oil on canvas, H. 29, W. 36-1/2 inches (73.7 x 92.7 cm.). Gift of Joseph H. Hazen, 1970. Acc.n.: 1970.305; Balthus, The Mountain, 1937, oil on canvas, H. 98, W. 144 in. (248.9 x 365.8 cm.). Purchase, Gifts of Mr. and Mrs. Nate B. Spingold and Nathan Cummings, Rogers Fund and The Alfred N. Punnett Endowment Fund, by exchange, and Harris Brisbane Dick Fund, 1982. Acc.n.: 1982.530; Ernst Max, The Barbarians, 1937 (dated), oil on cardboard, H. 9-1/2, W. 13 inches (24 x 33 cm.).Jacques and Natasha Gelman Collection, 1998. Acc.n.: 1999.363.21.Photo: Malcom Varon; Magritte Rene', Edward James in front of 'On the Threshold of Liberty', 1937, gelatin silver print, 10.8 x 16.7 cm (4 1/4 x 6 9/16 in.). Inscribed: Inscribed on print, verso C: ' 'Edward James (II) / devant 'Au Sevil // de la Liberte' '; stamped on print, verso C: '7 232'; inscribed on print, verso LL: 'MAGRITTE 4';. Ford Motor Company Collection, Gift of Ford Motor Company and John C. Waddell, 1987. Acc.n.: 1987.1100.157; Man Ray, Compass, 1920, gelatin silver print, 11.7 x 8.6 cm (4 5/8 x 3 3/8 in.). Inscribed: Signed and inscribed in pencil on mount, recto, below print, bottom left: 'Man Ray'; bottom right: '1920'.Ford Motor Company Collection, Gift of Ford Motor Company and John C. Waddell, 1987. Acc. n.: 1987.1100.40; Miro' Joan, Dutch Interior, 1928, oil on canvas, H. 51-1/8, W. 38-1/8 inches (129.9 x 96.8 cm.) . Bequest of Florene M. Schoenborn, 1995. Inv. 1996.403.8; Picasso Pablo, Dora Maar in an Armchair, 1939, oil on canvas, H. 28-7/8, W. 23-3/4 inches (73.3 x 60.3

cm.) . The Mr. and Mrs. Klaus G. Perls Collection, 1998. Inv. 1998.23; Dali' Salvador, Crucifixion (Corpus Hypercubus), 1954, oil on canvas, 1954. Gift of The Chester Dale Collection, 1955. Inv.55.5; Miro' Joan, Constellation: Women on the Beach; [Constellation: Femmes sur la Plage], 1940 (dated), gouache and oil wash on paper, 1940. Jacques and Natasha Gelman Collection, 1998. Inv.1999.363.52; Miro' Joan, Women and Bird at Night, 1944, gouache on canvas, 9 1/4 x 16 3/4' (23.5 x 42 cm). Jacques and Natasha Gelman Collection, 1998. Inv.1999.363.54. Photo: Malcolm Varon, Tanguy Yves, My Life, Black and White, 1944, oil on canvas, 1944. Jacques and Natasha Gelman Collection, 1998. Inv.1999.363.81; Tanguy Yves, From Green to White, 1954, oil on canvas, 99x81,3 cm. Jacques and Natasha Gelman Collection, 1998. Inv.1999.363.82.

THE MUSEUM OF MODERN ART, NEW YORK
Balthus, Joan Miro and His Daugther Dolores, 1937-38, oil on canvas, 51 1/4 x 35' (130.2 x 88.9 cm). Abby Aldrich Rockefeller Fund. 398.1938; Cornell Joseph, Untitled (Bebe' Marie), early 1940's, pape-red and painted wood box, with painted corrugated cardboard floor, containing doll in cloth dress and straw hat with cloth flowers, dried flowers, and twigs, flecked with paint, 23 1/2 x 12 3/8 x 5 1/4' (59.7 x 31.5 x 13.3 cm). Acquired through the Lillie P. Bliss Bequest. 682.1980; Dali' Salvador, Illuminated Pleasures, 1929, oil and collage on composition board, 9 3/8 x 13 3/4' (23.8 x 34.7 cm). The Sidney and Harriet Janis Collection. 584.1967; Kahlo Frida, My Grandparen-ts, My Parents, and I (Family Tree), 1936, oil and tempera on metal panel, 12 1/8 x 13 5/8' (30.7 x 34.5 cm). Gift of Allan Roos, M.D., and B. Mathieu Roos. Acc. n.: 277.1987.a-c.; Giacometti Alberto, Woman with Her Throat Cut (Femme egoree), 1932, bronze (cast 1949), 8 x 34 1/2 x 25' (20.3 x 87.6 x 63.5 cm). Purchase. 1; Oppenheim Meret, Object (Le dejeuner en fourrure), 1936, Fur-covered cup, saucer and spoon; cup, 4 3/8' (10.9 cm) diameter; saucer, 9 3/8' (23.7 cm) dia-meter; spoon, 8' (20.2 cm) long; overall height 2 7/8' (7.3 cm). Pur-chase. Acc. n.: 130.1946.a-c.; Matta Echaurren, Roberto Sebastian, The Vertigo of Eros (Le Vertige d'Eros), 1944, oil on canvas, 6' 5' x 8' 3' (195.6 x 251.5 cm). Given anonymously. 65.1944; Miro' Joan, Du-tch Interior I, 1928, oil on canvas, 36 1/8 x 28 3/4' (91.8 x 73 cm). Mrs. Simon Guggenheim Fund. 163.1945; Picabia Francis, Comic We-dlock (Mariage comique), c. June-July 1914, oil on canvas, 6' 5 3/8' x 6' 6 ¾ ' (196,5x2009 cm). Eugene and Agnes E. Meyer Collection, given by their family. 01409.74; Tanguy Yves, Extinction of Useless Lights (Extinction des lumieres inutiles), 1927, oil on canvas, 36 1/4 x 25 3/4' (92.1 x 65.4 cm). Purchase. 220.1936; Tanguy Yves, Slowly Toward the North (Vers le nord lentement), 1942, oil on canvas, 42 x 36' (106.7 x 91.4 cm). Gift of Philip Johnson. 627.1943; Arp Jean (Hans), Human Concretion, 1935, original plaster, 19 1/2 x 18 3/4 x 25 1/2' (49.5 x 47.6 x 64.7 cm). Gift of the Advisory Committee. 4.1937; Dali' Salvador, Retrospective Bust of a Woman (Buste de femme retrospectif), 1933, painted porcelain, bread, corn, feathers, paint on paper, beads, ink stand, sand and two pens, 29 x 27 1/4 x 12 5/8' (73.9 x 69.2 x 32 cm). Acquired through the Lillie P. Bliss Bequest and gift of Philip Johnson (by exchange). 301.1992; Ernst Max, The Gramineous Bicycle Garnished with Bells the Dappled Fire Damps and the Echinoderms Bending the Spine to Look for Caresses, 1920-21, botanical chart altered with gouache, 29 ¼ x 39 ¼ " (74,3x99,7 cm).

Purchase. 279.1937; Lam Wilfredo, The Jungle, 1943, gouache on paper mounted on canvas, 7' 10 ¼ " x 7' 6 ½ " (239.4 x 229.9 cm). Inter-American Fund. Acc. n.: 140.1945; Miro' Joan, Still Life with Old Shoe (Paris, January 24 - May 29 1937), oil on canvas, 32 x 46' (81,3x116,8 cm.). Gift of James Thrall Soby. 1094.1969; Picasso, Pa-blo, Goat Skull and Bottle (Vallauris, 1951), Painted bronze, (cast 1954) after an assemblage of bicycle handlebars, nails, metal and ceramic elements, 31 x 37 5/8 x 21 1/2' (78.8 x 95.3 x 54.5 cm). Mrs. Simon Guggenheim Fund. 272.1956; Balthus, Andre' Derain. 1936, oil on wood, 44 3/8 x 28 1/2' (112.7 x 72.4 cm). Acquired through the Lillie P. Bliss Bequest. 67.1944; Delvaux, Paul, Phases of the Moon {Les phases de la lune}. 1939, oil on canvas, 55 x 63' (139.7 x 160 cm). Purchase. 504.1951; Dali' Salvador, Portrait of Gala (L'Angelus de Gala). 1935, oil on wood, 12 3/4 x 10 1/2' (32.4 x 26.7 cm). Gift of Abby Aldrich Rockefeller. 298.1937; Picasso Pablo, Seated Bather, oil on canvas, 64 1/4 x 51' (163.2 x 129.5 cm). Mrs. Simon Guggenheim Fund. 82.1950; Balthus, The Street. 1933, oil on canvas, 6' 4 3/4' x 7' 10 1/2' (195 x 240 cm). James Thrall Soby Bequest. 12009.1979, Tan-guy Yves; Miro' Joan; Morise Max; Man Ray, 'Cadavre exquis': Nude, 1926-27, Composite drawing: pen and ink, pencil, and colored crayon on paper, 14 1/4 x 9 1/8' (36.2 x 22.9 cm.). Purchase. 260.1935; Ernst Max, Napoleon in the Wilderness, 1941, oil on canvas, 18 1/4 x 15' (46.3 x 38.1 cm). Purchase and exchange. 12.1942; Miro' Joan, The Hunter (Catalan landscape), 1923-24, oil on canvas, 25 1/2 x 39 1/2' (64.8 x 100.3 cm). Purchase. 95.1936; Breton Andre', Poem-Object, 1941, Assemblage mounted on wood drawing board: carved wood bust of man, oil lantern, framed photograph, toy boxing gloves, 18 x 21 x 4 3/8' (45.8 x 53.2x 10.9 cm). Kay Sage Tanguy Bequest. Acc. n.: 197.1963; Cornell Joseph, Object (Roses des vents), 1942-53, Woo-den box with 21 compasses set into a wooden tray resting on plexi-glass-topped-and-partitioned section, divided into 17 compartments containing small miscellaneous objects, and three-part hinged lid co-vered inside with parts of maps of New Guinea and Australia, 2 5/8 x 21 1/4 x 10 3/8' (6.7 x 53.7 x 26.2 cm). Mr. and Mrs. Gerald Murphy Fund. 621.1973.w1; Cornell Joseph, Object (Roses des vents), 1942-53, Wooden box with 21 compasses set into a wooden tray resting on plexiglass-topped-and-partitioned section, divided into 17 compart-ments containing small miscellaneous objects, and three-part hinged lid covered inside with parts of maps of New Guinea and Australia, 2 5/8 x 21 1/4 x 10 3/8' (6.7 x 53.7 x 26.2 cm). Mr. and Mrs. Gerald Murphy Fund. 621.1973.w2; Miro' Joan, The Carbide Lamp, 1922-23, Oil on canvas, 15 x 18' (38.1 x 45.7 cm.). Purchase. Acc. n.: 12.1939; Matta Echaurren, Roberto Sebastian, Malitte Lounge Furniture, 1966 (manufacturer: Knoll International, New York), Polyurethane foam and wool. Overall: 63 X 63 X 25 (160 X 160 X 63.5 cm). Gift of Knoll In-ternational. Acc. num. 473.1970.a-e; Matta Echaurren, Roberto Seba-stian, Malitte Lounge Furniture, 1966 (manufacturer: Knoll Internatio-nal, New York), Polyurethane foam and wool. Overall: 63 X 63 X 25 (160 X 160 X 63.5 cm). Gift of Knoll International. Acc. num. 473.1970. a-e; Horst, Horst Paul, Costume for Salvador Dali's 'Dream of Venus', c. 1939, gelatin silver print, 9 13/16 x 7 1/2 (25 x 19.1cm). Gift of James Thrall Soby. Acc. n.: 69.1993; Ernst Max, The Little Tear Gland that Says Tic Tac (inscribed: La petite fistule lacrimale qui dit tic tac), 1920, pen-cil and ink on stenciled wallpaper mounted on board with ink, 14 1/4 x 10'. Purchase. Acc. n.: 238.1935; Man Ray, Rayograph, 1922, gelatin silver print, 9 3/8 x 11 3/4' (23.9 x 30 cm). Gift of James Thrall Soby. Acc. n.: 110.1941; Miro' Joan, Still Life - Glove and Newspaper, 1921, oil on canvas, 46 x 35 1/4'. Gift of Armand G. Erpf. Acc. n.: 18.1955, Ernst Max, The King Playing with the Queen, 1944 (cast 1945), bronze, 38 1/2' high, 18 3/4 x 20 1/2' at base. Gift of D. and J. de Menil. Acc. n.: 330.1955, Man Ray, Marcel Proust on his death-bed, taken during the funeral eve, Monday, November 22nd, 1922; Picasso Pablo, Woman Dressing Her Hair, Royan, June 1940, oil on canvas, 51 1/4 x 38 1/4' (130.1 x 97.1 cm). Louise Reinhardt Smith Bequest. Acc. n.: 788.1995; Dali' Salvador, Untitled (Petit theatre), 1934, wood and glass, painted, 12 3/4 x 16 3/4 x 12 1/4' (32.3 x 42.5 x 31.1 cm). Acquired through the James Thrall Soby Bequest, and the Abby Aldrich Rockefeller, Loula D. Lasker, and William S. Paley Funds. Acc. n.: 57.1981; Ernst Max, 'Stratified Rocks, Nature's Gift of Gneiss Lava Iceland Moss 2 kinds of lungwort 2 kinds of ruptures of the perinaeum growths of the heart b) the same thing in a well-polished little box somewhat more expensive', 1920, gouache and pencil on chromolithograph mounted on board with ink inscriptions, 6 x 8 1/8' (15.2 x 20.6 cm). Purchase. Acc. n.: 280.1937; Arp, Jean (Hans), Constellation, 1932, painted wood, 11 3/4 x 13 1/8 x 2 3/8' (29.6 x 33.1 x 6 cm). The Sidney and Harriet Janis Collection. Acc. n.: 576.1967; Tanguy Yves, Untitled, 1936, decalcomania (ink transfer) on paper, 12 3/4 x 19 3/4' (32.5 x 50.2 cm). Alva Gimbel Fund. Acc. n.: 13.1969, Arp, Jean (Hans), Objets places d'apres la loi du hasard (Objects Arranged According to the Law of Chance), 1930, wood, 10 3/8 x 11 1/8 x 2 1/4' (26.3 x 28.3 x 5.4 cm.). Purchase. Acc. n.: 79.1936; Miro' Joan, peinture murale (Mural Painting). Barcelona, October 18th, 1950 - January 26th, 1951, oil on canvas, 6' 2 3/4' x 19' 5 3/4' (188.8 x 593.8 cm). Mrs. Simon Guggenheim Fund. Acc. n.: 592.1963; Arp, Jean (Hans), Mountain, Table, Anchors and Navel, 1925, gouache on board with cutouts, 29 5/8 x 23 1/2' (75.2 x 59.7 cm). Purchase. Acc. n.: 77.1936; Giacometti Alberto, Le Couple (The Couple), 1926, bronze, 23 1/2 x 14 1/2 x 7' (59.7 x 36.8 x 17.8 cm). Sylvia Slifka Bequest. Acc. n.: 21.20094; Giacometti Alberto, Femme-cuillere (Spoon Woman), 1926-27, bronze, 57 x 20 1/4 x 8 1/4' (144.8 x 51.4 x 21 cm). Acquired through the Mrs. Rita Silver Fund in honor of her husband Leo Silver and in memory of her son Stanley R. Silver, and the Mr. and Mrs. Walter Hochschild Fund. Acc. n.: 158.1986; Horst, Horst Paul, Costume for Salvador Dali's 'Dream of Venus', c. 1939, Gelatin silver print. 7 1/2 x 10 (19 x 25.4 cm). Gift of James Thrall Soby. Acc. num. 70.1993.